Introduction to Humans Moving

A Guide to Philosophy in Action

John M. Charles
The College of William and Mary

ISBN 1-58874-122-2

Published by

Stipes Publishing L.L.C.
204 W. University Ave.
Champaign, Illinois 61820

ACKNOWLEDGEMENTS

The publication of *Introduction to Humans Moving* has been a communal effort. The members of the three communities that I wish to thank were probably unaware of each other and of their impact on my writing. Yet, they each deeply influenced my scholarship.

First and foremost I am indebted to my family. My father and mother encouraged both my questioning mind and a love of words. My wife, Kelly, and children, Sean and Kendra, were (and still are) a constant support.

The second community that has made this book possible is The College of William and Mary. The college generously provided a faculty research assignment to allow me to write the manuscript. The students in my classes have offered constant feedback on the theory in the text and the practice of the applied philosophy exercises. Laura Hanson, who took all of the photographs, deserves the credit for the pictorial appearance of the book.

The final community to which I am indebted is the cadre of philosophers who have most shaped my worldview. Jan Broekhoff was the mentor for my doctoral studies at The University of Oregon. He introduced me to the notion that philosophy could be a vibrant practical search for knowledge. In the foreword to a book that influenced this text considerably, *The Philosophic Process in Physical Education* (written by William Harper, Donna Mae Miller, Roberta J. Park and Elwood Craig Davis and published by Lea and Febiger in 1977), Jan Broekhoff summarizes our shared approach. We agree that we should "reject the 'philosophy of the ivory tower' and opt for the primacy of the act – the act of doing and the act of thinking." Another contemporary scholar who has influenced me through his emphasis on the dynamic nature of the philosophic search is Scott Kretchmar. He clearly outlines the applied and personal nature of the search in *Practical Philosophy of Sport (Human Kinetics, 1994)* and encourages the student to participate in the art and science of the philosophic process. Finally, Seymour Kleinman has focussed my attention more on the art than the science of our existence. He has encouraged the many individuals who have been influenced by his ideas to live life as an artist. I have tried to follow his advice in this book.

Table of Contents

Preface vii

PART I: THE PHILOSOPHIC METHOD 1

    Chapter 1: The Philosophic Method 3
        Preview
        Introduction to Philosophy in our World 3
        Action in Philosophy 7
        Review and Preview 17
        Philosophy in Action 18
        Review 29

PART II: DEVELOPING UNDERSTANDING 31

    Chapter 2: Self - Understanding 33
        Preview 33
        Understanding Self-understanding 33
        Self-Understanding Through Movement 38
        Body of Knowledge 42
        Living Through The Body 45
        Review and Preview 51
        Earning A Living Through The Body 52
        Review 64

    Chapter 3: Understanding Others 65
        Preview 65
        Encountering Eastern Philosophy 66
        Review and Preview 69
        Implications of Eastern Philosophy for Western Society 69
        Applications of Eastern Philosophy in Western Society 72
        The Art and Science of Movement and Medicine 80
        Review 84

PART III: LIVING THE GOOD LIFE

Chapter 4: Playing 87
    Preview 87
    The Promise of Play 87
    The Elements of Play 88
    Play as Not-Work 93
    Play and Sport 96
    Review and Preview 98
    Why People Play 99
    Play As You Grow 103
    Why Live Your Life As Play? 107
    Why Live A Culture's Life As Play? 113
    Review 115

Chapter 5: Appreciating Movement 117
    Preview 117
    The Art and Science of Movement 117
    Sport As Art 118
    Sport As Aesthetic 121
    Experiencing the Aesthetic 122
    Expressing the Aesthetic 126
    Evaluating the Aesthetic 129
    Review 130

PART IV: CHOOSING THE RIGHT PATH 131

Chapter 6: Making Moral Choices 133
    Preview 133
    The Growing Need for Ethics 133
    How To Make Ethical Decisions 139
    Review and Preview 146
    Putting Theory into Practice 147
    Justice and Equality in Education, Sport and Healthcare 148
    Individual Autonomy and Paternalism 151
    Conclusion: Live the Good Life 157
    Review 158

PREFACE

This book presents and represents the human side of movement study. As introductory texts become increasingly empirical and scientific, this book stands alone as a tribute to the human values in contemporary kinesiology. It provides an overview of the lifetime skills that can be developed through human movement study. It not only provides a framework for critical thinking, but it also involves you, the reader, in the process. Unlike many books written for use in college classes, this one should not be discarded when the class is over. Although the ideas may be presented in a class setting, they provide a framework for life.

This book is written with your growth and development very much in mind. It is a valuable companion reader to any of the introductory texts currently on the market. They may provide the knowledge and skills you need to enter graduate schools and the professions, but they do not focus on your self-development. Human growth, which should be the essence of higher education, cannot take place without self-examination. This book places you at the center of the educational process. It gives you the opportunity to look at yourself as a moving being, to understand who you are and where you are in your life.

The key used to unlock your inner self is philosophy. If the word "philosophy" has negative connotations, *Introduction to Humans Moving* will increase your comfort level with the term. Philosophy is presented as being an action-packed search for wisdom that will bring more meaning to your life. The concepts and skills described in this book are eminently useful. They have application beyond the academic realm. These are the tools necessary to transform our culture, to enhance our education system, to give life vibrancy and vigor. They are not only abstract and cerebral concepts, but they also give movement and its study purpose and personal meaning.

The term kinesiology is used throughout the text to describe human movement study because it is the label being adopted most universally to define the field. Since the American Academy of Kinesiology and Physical Education proclaimed in 1989 that kinesiology should become the one nationally recognized descriptor for the academic study of human movement, there has been a gradual, but perceptible, shift in that direction. Kinesiology is becoming a more popular name than Physical Education because it is a more inclusive title. It represents the changing emphasis of the field away from the traditional single-minded emphasis on teacher preparation towards new professional directions. At the dawn of the new millenium, kinesiology programs are expanding beyond their traditional professional preparation emphases on teaching and sport-related careers to embrace such burgeoning opportunities as preventive, complementary and traditional medicine, health awareness and promotion, physical literacy and efficiency and lifetime skills and exercise habits. Both of these names, philosophy and kinesiology, denote opportunity. They certainly both have a history but this book is more about how, when linked together, they can lead into the future.

The book is appropriate as a reading in an introduction to kinesiology class, or as a basic text for a philosophy course, or as a focus of discussion in issues and principles courses. It is written at an appropriate level for all undergraduate students, so it is ideally suited for an introductory class where goals of the course include examining reasons for selecting this major and considering career options. Given this emphasis on personal assessment and future directions, junior and senior class majors with a background in the field and more intellectual maturity will find this reading most rewarding. The questions raised throughout the text are thought provoking enough to be suitable for an issues-oriented graduate seminar.

The approach is designed to challenge you to consider your purpose, to think about why you are attracted to movement and it's study and to examine what you value in your choice of a profession. It is more about the philosophic process than about the formal content of philosophy. It is about attitudes that you hold toward your physical being, your daily movement activities and your future. Above all this book is about **you,** about becoming a clear thinker and a purposeful mover.

To help you in this process, each chapter contains a series of exercises that will challenge you to think about important philosophic issues. These exercises have been "road-tested" by college students. Their responses are included as a counter-point to your own thinking. Previews and reviews act as guideposts to the text within each chapter.

The book is designed to take you on a journey through your own mind. At each of the several stops along the way, you will gather the necessary information to reach your ultimate destination. If you can arrive at an understanding of what meaning you find in your body and your movement, if you can make sense of why you are attracted to this field of study and if you can develop a sense of purpose your journey will have been worthwhile.

Because you will encounter dangerous and troubling issues as you venture through previously unexplored terrain, you must be armed for the struggle. The armory where you will receive the weapons and ammunition of philosophy is the necessary point of departure. In the first chapter you will be equipped with the skills of philosophy. You will be challenged to go beyond handling these weapons to practicing firing blanks, so that when you encounter the substantive questions of the later chapters you will know how to proceed. Throughout the book, you will have the opportunity to step beyond book knowledge into the realm of experience. Through exercises that you tackle in each section, you will infuse abstract philosophic concepts with meanings that are based in your own lived reality.

The station at which you will next alight: **self-understanding**, is a major terminus for philosophy. It is obviously imperative that you evaluate who you are, before you proceed to consider who you may become. The particular emphasis of this section is how you know yourself as a physical being. The question of the mind-body relationship is critical, not only for you on your personal philosophic journey, but also for the field of kinesiology. Both the study of the discipline in the university and the practice of professions that focus on the human body are deeply affected by the answer to this question.

Your philosophic journey would be incomplete if it was landlocked in our cultural perspective. Developing human beings throughout the world are travelling along similar, but different paths to their philosophical destinations. Becoming philosophically mature is a universal enterprise, which is marked by significant regional variations. These variations are more than matters of style. They are the substance of ideology, of prevailing ways of thinking and of religious custom. Our philosophic self-development would be stunted if we took a culturally myopic pathway through our movement studies. The next chapter is designed to help you in **understanding others** by encountering belief-systems and practices that are traditionally eastern. The readings and exercises encourage you to not only understand alternative perspectives, but also to think about their implications for your philosophy and their applications in your practice.

Continuing on your philosophic journey, you will be required to make a couple of stops to examine what you find to be valuable in your own personal movement experiences and how these qualities contribute to **the good life**. Thinking about **playing** and **appreciating human movement** can lead you to a better understanding of what constitutes happiness, in general, and, more particularly, what makes you happy when you move. Playing is a critical process in the formation of our creative capacities. In society, and most particularly in our educational institutions, playing is viewed in relation to working. It may be an outcome of work (we work to be able to find time and earn money to play) or it may be opposed to work (study versus recess, or work versus vacation), but it is usually relegated to a secondary status. In many ways our field of study is uniquely capable of featuring and focussing on play as a cultural phenomenon and as a meaningful personal process. In this chapter you will be challenged to consider play as a theoretical construct and to practice playing in such a way that it may contribute in fulfilling ways to your sense of wellbeing.

Appreciating the human body and the movement process falls within the philosophical domain of aesthetics. Society rewards efficiency, time management and economy of effort. We tend to be utilitarian in our purpose in that we move to complete a task or perhaps to win. Human movement can be conducted in that utilitarian mode, but it is also a realm of beauty. The human body and physical activity have been a focus of art through the ages. In many cases, you may have been attracted to movement (and perhaps to its study) by the sense of beauty, joy and happiness that moving brought to your life. This chapter provides a theoretical framework for understanding the aesthetic dimensions of human movement. More importantly, it involves you in using that framework to experience, express and evaluate the beauty in your own movement experiences.

Opportunity necessitates choice. At the dawning of the new millennium, you are faced with a world of opportunity that exceeds the wildest visions of previous generations. Globalization, technology and peaceful prosperity are three trends that have contributed to the landscape you are entering on your philosophic journey. This terrain is an ethical minefield. At every turn, you must decide what is **the right path**. **Making moral choices** is not an option in tomorrow's world. Given that you will have to make ethical decisions, you will be better prepared if you are aware of some of the dilemmas that may confront you and if you have prepared and practiced ways to resolve them. This chapter outlines some of the ethical dilemmas that you will face in the human movement field and provides a framework for ethical decision making. The discussion is punctuated by a series of exercises and ethical case studies that will challenge you to test your ethical decision-making skills in real-life situations. By the end of this unit, you should understand ethical theory and be able to apply it by choosing the best course of action as moral dilemmas confront you.

This final chapter is the culmination of your philosophic journey. Without the critical thinking skills of philosophy, people tend to wander through life. Things happen to them, they are innocent victims of circumstances. Much like electricity, they tend to take the path of least resistance through their life-journey. Philosophy, developed through the processes described in this book, provides a compass to help you through the vicissitudes of your existence. Rather than finding yourself in the position of always dealing with the unexpected, you can become adept at analyzing and synthesizing. The skills that you have developed will allow you to chart a course and to respond predictably and reasonably to future events.

This book, then, will introduce you to life skills, skills that are as essential to your health and wellbeing as the fitness-based skills developed in the gymnasium or as critical to your understanding as the knowledge-based skills you may encounter in the classroom. Through reading and using this text you will be

Developing understanding

- Of self through consideration of mind and body relationships
- Of others through consideration of self and other relationships as we encounter foreign ideas in the movement of non-western cultures

Living the good life

- through emphasizing play

- through appreciating beauty in and through our movement

Choosing the right path

- through differentiating right from wrong in movement-related settings.

These are lifetime skills that will take a lifetime to develop. They are the philosophic foundations of the study of humans moving that are a vital necessity in today's society. Although they augment the science-based study of the body and motion with a philosophical examination of the human dimension, they are not always emphasized in the kinesiology curriculum. In light of Socratic wisdom that an unexamined life is not worth living, this philosophic self-examination belongs in every program of study that values quality of life as highly as the transmission of knowledge.

Part I

THE PHILOSOPHIC METHOD

Chapter 1
THE PHILOSOPHIC METHOD

Preview

This chapter is designed to help you to answer the following fundamental questions:

1. What is philosophy?

2. Why is it important for me to become more philosophical?

3. What does this process entail?

4. What does applied philosophy mean?

5. What is the relationship between my philosophy and my movement?

The applications of philosophy are in your everyday existence. Your philosophy determines your attitudes, your values, what you choose to do and who your friends are. Philosophy is the love of wisdom. It is an intellectual and personal search. It involves asking questions and developing answers that will lead to a course of action.

Introduction to Philosophy in our World

To get started on this search, consider each of the following pairs of scenarios of contrasting opinions. They will become the focus of the exercises that follow. These paired statements and the subsequent exercises are designed to prepare you from the outset to recognize the impact of philosophy. This process involves recognizing the diversity of opinions on topics important to our field and in picking your own path between the extremes.

The Education Scene

1. Education is the key to social mobility. Socially disadvantaged children have every opportunity of fulfilling their potential through the free public schooling and the many entitlement programs available to them. Since the passage of laws designed to protect the rights of minorities, females and those with disabling conditions, discriminatory practices have effectively been eliminated from the nation's schools. An increasing emphasis on learning goals and accountability for meeting those goals is producing a more efficient and effective school curriculum. Teaching is a secure profession that provides a comfortable wage and the feeling of wellbeing associated with a career that revolves around helping others to grow and to learn.

2. Education is in a state of crisis. Functional illiteracy is rampant, dropout rates are high and enthusiasm for learning is low, particularly among minority youth. Judging from a series of comparative studies, American children are learning less through their schooling than their European counterparts. Teaching is a low status profession. There is a perception that the least able students choose teaching as a career. In times of need, schools hire poorly qualified teachers. Sometimes aggressive minority recruitment erodes the quality of the teaching force. In schools discipline standards are lax, teachers are often more concerned with maintaining order than facilitating learning. Disillusionment among teachers is common. Many seek jobs elsewhere.

The Physical Education Scene

1. Increasing public awareness about the importance of fitness, the risks of obesity and the value of exercise augur well for physical education in the schools. Because children are naturally active and enjoy many movement experiences, they should find physical education to be an attractive and rewarding alternative to other "dry" school subjects. Recent initiatives in the curriculum, which emphasize clearly achievable fitness goals, bring physical education in line with other school disciplines that are seeking clearer definition of learning goals, more measurable outcomes and more accountability. Teaching physical education must be a very rewarding career. Not only do you get job security and a decent working wage, you also get to do what you want to do as a profession - play games, share your movement interests with enthusiastic children and know that you are helping to create a fitter, healthier nation.

2. Physical education in schools is a shambles. Without any shared mission, physical education programs range from being an adjunct to athletics to being glorified recess. Meanwhile, the nation's children become more sedentary, more obese, more at-risk. Those who enjoy sport and whose parents can afford to pay for the experience look to community programs for their exercise, the others languish in front of the television. Although most children enjoy physical activity when

they are young they are generally "turned off" exercise by school physical education. The curricular emphasis on physical fitness achievement testing rewards physical prowess but stigmatizes those who cannot perform. It certainly does little to cultivate joy in movement. Teachers are often coaches, many of whom are more concerned with athletic successes than cultivating the physical skills of their less able students. Morale is low because of budget cuts, reduced graduation requirements for physical education and student requirements.

The Kinesiology Scene

1. Kinesiology is on the crest of a wave. The time is ripe for kinesiology programs to flourish in universities across the nation. In response to public and political pressure, higher education is more closely aligning itself with societal needs. Kinesiology clearly has a niche in this process. The nation wants a better health care system, more education in prevention, wellness and nutrition, better public schools, better athletes and more records on the sports field and more of a focus on aging gracefully and actively without debilitating injury. Kinesiology can help to meet these needs. Now that it has shed its dependence upon Athletics in most universities, it has developed a discipline-based curriculum and research agenda, it is populated by scholars with doctorates, rather than teacher-coaches and it is preparing to take its rightful place in the upper echelons of the university power structure.

2. Remember Washington, Oregon, Missouri? These are only the forerunners of a host of programs that will be a victim of the budget-cutters, restructuring axes. There is no agreement on a mutual mission in the field. Why, programs have been fighting for a hundred years over what to call themselves and still can't agree! While the field is in such disarray kinesiology is vulnerable not only to downsizing but also to the slings and arrows of public opinion. Debate on the topic in Academe is sprinkled with such questions as

    - What is this new listing in the course handbook?

    - P.E. under a new name?

    - Biomechanics?

    - Is it science?

    - What can a student do with it?

    - Is it legitimate or is it a safe place for athletes without academic aspirations to hide?

Because it cannot clearly establish it's identity on campus and because professors cannot reach unanimity it will be peripheral to the mission of the university and will be one of the first programs to go in a budget crunch.

The Health Scene

1. America has the most advanced medical system in the world. There are plenty of doctors. They are well trained to treat every ailment using state-of-the-art technology and medicine. More money is spent in this country than anywhere else in the world (in absolute and per capita terms) on ensuring the healing and comfort of citizens. There is a growing awareness of the importance of prevention as an integral part of personal health, which is leading to the popularity of wellness programs in various settings. Doctors generally know what is in the best interests of their patients and tend to their wellbeing through a range of modalities.

2. The bottom line in the medical community today is economic self - interest. The basic premise of managed care is to minimize complications and to maximize profits. Without the appropriate insurance a growing minority of Americans can't get treatment for their ailments. Doctors are trained to be narrowly focused on chemical and surgical modes of a cure and tend to be resistant to complementary forms of treatment such as acupuncture, massage therapy and herbs. The personal touch of the family physician is becoming obsolete. Patients are shuttled in and out of the multiple practice clinics as quickly as possible. They often do not see their own primary care physician or get referred to a doctor who can actually treat their condition [particularly by unconventional methods]. There is virtually no prospect of any doctor paying them a home visit when they get too sick to travel to the clinic. Medical treatment is overpriced, alternative methods are underutilized, good care is accessible to the rich but not to the poor, physicians are in it for the money and don't really care about their patients.

The Sports Scene

1. Sport is a form of play through which we build character. Sportsmanship, teamwork, loyalty, grace in victory and dignity in defeat, leadership and courage are examples of values inculcated through sport. Sport is a melting pot that accepts all-comers, discriminating between them on the basis of athletic talent but ignoring race, class and gender distinctions. Sport is organized by the people for the people. It is an avenue of social mobility. Through the reward system of athletic scholarships, underprivileged students may earn acceptance to college to represent their school on the playing field and gain a high-quality education. Professional sport is a showcase of the best natural talent in the world.

2. If sport teaches any values at all, they are dysfunctional in today's world. Aggression, violence, the aggrandizement of power, uniformity, conformity and mindless subordination to authority figures are the moral foundation of many sports program. There is no dignity in losing. If you don't win, you may as well not play, so it doesn't really matter how you win, just so long as you do! Social mobility through athletic talent is a mirage - you're more likely to be struck by

lightening than rise through the ranks to fame and fortune. Untold numbers of underprivileged youth have found only disillusionment in their quest for athletic greatness. Many of the fortunate few who get college scholarships are exploited, suffer injury that haunts them for the rest of their lives, are shunted into easy [not necessarily rewarding] majors and often fail to graduate. Few of these athletes would claim that they are playing at sport - for them it is work. Sport is a hegemonic system that serves to reinforce the discrimination and prejudices of society. Cheating, corruption and performance-enhancing drug use are rapidly becoming the norm.

Action in Philosophy

Philosophic thinking may be sedentary in nature, but it is a most vigorous form of cerebral activity. It is a dynamic process of thinking through an issue. In this section you will follow a series of steps designed to help you to reach a higher level of philosophic maturity. The approach we will take is action-oriented and personalized. The action centers on a series of exercises. Just as when you go to a gym to work out, you do not expect to get much out of your exercises if you are not physically active, so it goes with these philosophic exercises. Your personal development is dependent upon the quality of your input.

You can tackle them on your own, with a partner, in a small group or even as a whole class. As the number of people working on these exercises together grows, the value of the return will diminish. Philosophical thinking is essentially a solitary business. Not that a philosopher must be a hermit, for philosophers are often thinking about people and given the nature of modern social existence, they usually find themselves in a crowd. Few of us can be, or even want to be, like William Wordsworth who was able to bask in the solitude of his native environment, walking the hills and dales of the Lake District, thinking deeply and composing poems to communicate his ideas. We can rarely afford to distance ourselves from society in order to think. Perhaps we don't really want to. But, whether in the company of others or alone, a prerequisite of attaining philosophic maturity is that you must be thinking **for yourself**. Large groups tend to intimidate, to stifle independent thinking and to transform problem solving into an experience in social dynamics. Instead of thinking through an issue yourself at your own pace you will probably be swept up in a whirlwind of opinion, agreeing with one point of view, getting upset at another, wanting to reach a consensus, not wishing to be unpopular. To successfully complete these exercises, try to put yourself in a setting where you can think through an issue in your own way and share your conclusions without feeling threatened.

Exercise 1-1: Reacting

From the pairs of scenarios above, pick a topic that you find interesting. Read both opinions about that scene and answer the following questions:

- which of these positions seems to be closest to your way of thinking?

- what are the ideas that you particularly agree with?

- how does the other paired sentence make you feel? Why?

Discussion: Welcome to the world of philosophy! You have now embarked upon a journey toward greater self-understanding. You have taken the first step beyond blind acceptance (which is the condition that characterizes the severely philosophically challenged!). You have read and thought about two somewhat conflicting opinions. You have experienced varying degrees of doubt and skepticism about some of the things that you read. These doubts are often the springboards that will propel you into the depths of philosophy. From initial reservations a search may take form: a search for truth, for plausible alternatives to positions you doubt, for wisdom. This willingness to embark on a quest for truth is the essential starting point of philosophy. Only if you will to look can you expect to find - not only acceptable answers, but also a love of the process of seeking truth. This "love of wisdom" is the literal meaning of philosophy and fostering it is the purpose of this book.

Dangers: This first important step forward into the world of philosophy should be taken with trepidation. The trail toward wisdom is neither straight nor easily navigable. Like the pilgrims journeying down the trail to the Promised Land in Pilgrims Progress (written by John Bunyan), you will encounter many hazards en route. The first of these is a tendency to be <u>overconfident</u>. It may be tempting to claim that because you have read and reacted to two position statements you are now philosophizing. After all everyone else does (public figures seem to have philosophies about almost every topic, ranging from the purpose of their existence to which soap brand is better). The word, philosophy is often loosely used to connote opinion, idea or theory, but its errant public usage should not be a roadblock in your own personal journey. Philosophic thought may start on the surface like other more shallow forms of thinking but from there it proceeds past the skin-deep level to answer questions that focus on what humans should do, be and strive for, the meaning of life and the quality of existence.

A second ever-present danger lurking behind the initial-reaction approach to philosophy is "the feelings trap". Strong emotional responses can be inhibiting to clear thinking. The wording of the third question in Exercise 1 was designed to accentuate this pitfall. "How do you feel" is a more appropriate phrase in psychological counseling than in a philosophy text because in philosophy we seek to harness our feelings in order to think and act in a deliberate, detached way. Our emotional reaction to an issue is often immediate and visceral, but our philosophic response should be careful and profound. Can philosophers be passionate beings? Of course! It is not necessary to be" a cold fish" to love wisdom. Many of the most profound thinkers pursue truth with a passion that attests to deeply held beliefs, but in order to discern the wood from the trees they must curb their feelings. Deep thoughts and wise action, not shallow passion, are basic to philosophy.

A third hazard for the novice philosopher is implied in the title of this section. Becoming more philosophic entails moving from the stage of reacting to the state of being pro active. Like electricity, the least philosophical of individuals may be expected to flow aimlessly and thoughtlessly along the path of least resistance. At the next stage, neophyte philosophers learn to recognize issues and to respond to them as they arise. It is during this stage that life seems to be happening to you, life seems to be beyond your control, the big picture is murky. It isn't until you reach philosophical maturity that you are able to anticipate, to reason and understand, to place events and ideas in a larger context, to be pro active.

Exercise 1-2: Self-Distancing

In this exercise look at all of the paired statements and respond to the following questions:

1. Which statement in each pair seems more critical?

2. What other labels would you use to distinguish one set of statements from the other?

3. Which set of claims is the "best fit" with your worldview?

4. What are the features of this set that you find most appealing?

5. Can you identify elements of the other set of views that contain an element of truth?

Discussion: One instructive way to understand this process is through an analogy with coaching. How is a coach uniquely positioned to help an athlete? One answer to this question is, of course, that coaches are a one-step removed from the action. As they are not caught up in the sweat and turmoil of the contest, they have a more distanced perspective. They witness the ebb and flow of momentum, the strengths and weaknesses of each player and can craft a strategy to win accordingly. In a sense, this is philosophy in action. In the cerebral world of ideas the same strategy will reap dividends. By stepping back, taking a deep breath and thinking an issue through, you can avoid the dangers of emotional interference, reaching hasty conclusions and failing to see the bigger picture. The exercise you have just completed asks you to perform the process of self-distancing. You stepped back from the one question that was your initial focus in order to make comparisons between a cluster of statements. You proceeded to look more closely at the common denominators and to introspectively match these underlying features with your own ideology. Finally, the exercise presented you with the opportunity to search for truth in views that you do not personally espouse. Each of these techniques, when practiced often can help to lead you to a state of philosophic detachment. This will allow you to scratch beneath the surface of an issue, to identify the elements of truth in competing claims and to see beyond the immediate foreground toward the big picture on the horizon.

Dangers: The athlete thinks he was fouled, the opposing coach saw it differently, the action replay interpreted by expert analysts in the booth was inconclusive. Each of the entities in this scenario is one step further removed from the action. The perspective on the play gets broader at each juncture as the distance from the immediate confrontation increases. However, even at the furthest point, interpretation of the event is colored by the limitations of information provided about the event [camera angles, etc.] and the foibles of human perception [for example, commentator bias]. Similarly, it is impossible to become so detached from a philosophic issue that true objectivity can be attained. Even scientific research, which may appear to be objective, is affected by human bias, so certainly the more woolly areas of investigation that go beyond science [which is the literal meaning of metaphysics] will contain an element of subjectivity. One of the products of the philosophic process is healthy skepticism, so that, paradoxically, even as you learn to distance yourself, your awareness that you can never truly detach yourself increases. You will learn to question objectivity claims, to examine the premises underlying scientific hypotheses and conclusions and to recognize the fallibility of human judgement. So, although self-distancing is desirable in philosophy and novices in the field should strive to attain it, it would be dangerous to ever expect to be, or claim to be, truly objective.

Exercise 1-3: Identifying

1. Study and briefly define in your own words what each of the following list of ten philosophic issues means:

   Human nature [good / bad]

   Human existence [purpose / meaning]

   Human values [virtues / vices]

   Moral being [right / wrong]

   Social being [duties / responsibilities]

   Change [nature / consequences]

   Justice [cause / effect]

   Freedom [liberty / determinism]

   Happiness [personal / utilitarianism]

   Beauty [recognition / experience]

2. Can you design a question that you might ask in everyday conversation for each of these philosophic topics?

3. Can you find an example of each of these philosophic topics in the paired statements?

4. To which of these topics are the most frequent allusions in the statements?

5. What do your reactions to the statements tell you about your views on each of these topics?

Discussion: Beneath the seemingly placid surface of even the most innocuous statements there lies a veritable treasure trove of sunken meaning. The process of becoming philosophically mature entails moving from shallow awareness to profound recognition. When you encountered exercise three, you became familiar with a partial list of philosophical questions. It may have surprised you that these issues were embedded in statements about aspects of everyday existence. As we proceed down this path together, I expect that this initial source of surprise will be replaced by recognition that a greater source of astonishment would be any statement that was not based on a philosophic premise. Every thought, every reflective action, the nature of your being and the quality of your relationships emanate from your philosophy of life. A reason to pursue this process of philosophic growth is to learn to identify the specifics of your own belief-system, to transform taken-for-granted assumptions into examined principles.

Dangers: The process of introspective identification is socially dangerous. It may transform an individual from the ever-popular social foil to a self-actualizing principled person. Social foils mirror the actions of those around, parrot their words and parody their behavior. They tend to be popular and successful precisely because they don't think for themselves, they always fits in with everyone else's plans and they can be persuaded to do almost anything. After disciplined self-distancing and careful examination of underlying principles, such individuals might make some decisions that would jeopardize their popularity (based on malleability). This process leads to self-awareness, to independent thinking and to principled action. Do you think the risks associated with this danger are worth taking?

Exercise 1-4: Analyzing

There is a range of approaches that can be used in the process of philosophic analysis, including:

Comparing

Contrasting

Criticizing

Examining

Exploring

Inspecting

Investigating

Probing

Scrutinizing

Differentiate between them, then use these analytical tools to conduct a microanalysis of a phrase in one of the statements [for example, "sports is a form of play"]. Proceed through the analysis by answering the following questions:

1. What do the words in the statement mean? Check each word for ambiguity, contradictions, inaccurate usage, double meanings, etc.

2. What do the words tell you about the author's purpose?

3. What values are implied in this statement?

4. How valid and reliable do you consider this phrase to be?

5. If this statement were shown to be true, what would be its consequence?

6. What are the presuppositions on which this phrase is based?

7. In what ways does this statement conflict and/or agree with what you know about this topic?

Discussion: Analysis is the heart of the philosophic process. In earlier exercises you practiced moving beyond the stage of reacting to distance yourself sufficiently from an issue that you can identify philosophical premises of an argument. The process of discovery culminates in critical analysis that takes various forms. You conducted a form of linguistic analysis when you differentiated between words that describe the process and again when you looked closely at a phrase you selected. You observed, no doubt, that similar words have slightly different shades of meaning, which can be manipulated by a skilful speaker to portray an issue in a certain light. Words sometimes seem to take on a life of their own. In theory they are our primary means of communication, but in practice they frequently serve to obscure or pervert our meaning. How often do you find yourself involved in conversations that revolve around such phrases as, "but, I didn't mean . . . " or," what I meant to say was . . . ". We can lose our meaning in the words we select, we can be persuaded by the adroit choice of words and we can even create new meanings by the way we piece words together in poetry and in everyday parlance. As your philosophical dexterity develops, you will become more metaphysically adept. Metaphysics deal with the nature of reality. You took the first step into this branch of philosophy when you attempted to define the words and encounter their reality as part of this exercise. Of course, metaphysics are much more than word games. Beyond the words lay a wealth of concepts that can be examined using logic or such forms of philosophic investigation as phenomenology, (which involves the discovery of conceptual essence through eidetic reduction).

To this point, the process of philosophizing may have seemed to be solitary - just you embarking on a search for wisdom. Nothing could be further from the truth. The philosophic pathway is a bustling highway teeming with the greatest minds our civilization has produced. Critical analysis is informed by this wealth of wisdom. Working in an intellectual vacuum, you may progress to a point, but to reach your philosophic potential you must consult the wisdom of the ages. Individual philosophers and schools of thought can help you to understand more fully. As we proceed to think about applied philosophy of movement in this book, you will be introduced to some of these resources.

Dangers: Analyzing can be a destructive process. It entails systematically shredding an argument, poking holes in a theory and questioning your own assumptions and beliefs. The better you get at it, the more the walls of your preconceived reality will crumble. On the one hand, critical theory is essential to the growth process. Many philosophers have spent their life ripping up the ideas of others and, by ridiculing such notions as that the world is flat, have advanced civilization. On the other hand, if you are so successful at analyzing that your old unexamined world crumbles to ruins at your feet, you may experience feelings of emptiness, (or what some existential philosophers have called angst or anomie). There is no need to be daunted at the prospect, however, because although the heart of the philosophic process is questioning, criticizing and analyzing, the soul is building, unifying and synthesizing.

Exercise 1-5: Synthesizing

Select one pair of scenario statements and proceed as follows:

1. Create a summary cluster of key words and concepts from the position you find most acceptable.

2. Study the alternative position, draw from it any notions that you agree with and create a new conceptual cluster.

3.   Consider what the sentences do not say on the topic and make a third cluster of key words to remind you of concepts that should be examined in this context.

4.   Combine the clusters to create your own philosophy on the topic. 20-30 words

Discussion: In this exercise, you had to move beyond the reaction stage and distance yourself from the sentences to consider the topic as a whole. Your first task was to identify key words and phrases and then to distinguish between levels of truth as you adopted some and discarded others. In order to complete the second task of sifting through the opposing position to find a statement you could make your own, you had to distance yourself from an argument that you might have found distasteful at first glance. Recognizing truth wherever it may appear, even in the words of an opponent, is a crucial element of synthesis. Next, you had to step away from the text and marshal all of the resources at your disposal to take a larger view of the topic. Your access to this resource pool of accumulated wisdom of unfathomable depth will increase as you read, discuss and encounter new ideas, new theories and new schools of thought. Having collected together all the information necessary to synthesize your philosophy, you were asked to unify the clusters into one constellation of ideas. This is not a simple process. You have to look beneath the surface for connected ideas and, when you find them, weave them together into an acceptable whole. Eliminating contradictions and inconsistencies takes time, thinking through what you really believe can be exhausting, but as Socrates so profoundly stated, "the unexamined life is not worth living."

Dangers: Synthesizing a philosophy is a lifelong journey along an arduous and perilous path. It takes time and effort. Recognizing truth in opposing positions, being aware that for every point there is a counterpoint and being open to acknowledging and even embracing a different conclusion is often difficult, but it is impossible to reach philosophical maturity if you are close-minded. You are trading the bliss of ignorance, of unexamined beliefs, biases and prejudices for a lifetime of challenge. Only through this process will you be all that you can be!

Review and Preview

At this juncture, let's conduct a perception check to see where we are in our philosophic journey. In the preceding pages we have examined the skills required to develop a personal philosophy. This investigation has been "hands on" in the sense that you have conducted your own analysis, reached your own conclusions and developed your own philosophic maturity. Already you have been introduced to a basic premise of this book: that philosophy is not your own philosophy until you experience it for yourself. Until you know it, feel it and do it, it is someone else's world-view. You may appropriate ideas from others to help form your philosophy, but it only becomes yours when you live it. The exercises were designed to facilitate this "lived philosophy" approach to the basic skills of the philosophic process. In the next section, we will proceed beyond the question of how philosophy is applied to introduce the element of movement. We will see how the skills associated with the world of ideas are critical to success in our movement endeavors. This will lead to the construction of your own movement philosophy. Finally we will take an introductory look at the unique understandings to be gained through philosophy that are so critical to the growth of our field of study, of our professions and ultimately, of you!

Philosophy in Action

The Meaning in Movement

As you glance at this title with your newly sharpened skills of critical analysis, you might be tempted to be skeptical and to question its basic premise. You might say something along the lines of, "how can the world of ideas affect our physical existence?" Such incredulity is common. After all, we have been brought up to believe that the mind and body are separate entities that operate in different spheres of learning. If you did raise such a reservation, examine and change the dualistic premise of your own question. To do so discard the Cartesian notion that we are bifurcated beings in which there is no connection between the mind learning and the body acting and substitute instead the idea that we learn through experience

Exercise 1-6: Self-assessment

To check your beliefs on this subject, let's see how you do on this little test:

- do you find meaning in your own, direct, sensory perception of yourself?

- do you experience yourself as significant during any movement activity?

- do you express your creativity in unique ways through the medium of movement?

- does movement help you to develop a personalized relationship with an impersonal world?

- do you learn about yourself and your environment through your movement experiences?

Discussion: If you answered yes on any of these questions, it would appear that your movement is more significant than the mere physical motion of your body. It is quite possible, however, that the quality of this significance is difficult, perhaps impossible, to explain. The quality of movement is ineffable. How do you describe the aroma of coffee, the feeling of silk, the taste of a fine wine, the sight of a sunset or the sensation of kicking, spiking, throwing or hitting a ball just right? Words cannot capture the magnificence of the moment. Similarly, because we have been taught to embrace the scientific method as a means of determining truth, we tend to accept the evidence of research and dismiss the immeasurable. However, tests cannot evaluate meaning in movement. What you get out of your activity is personal. It is yours to know and nobody else's to understand. We can measure fitness gains and fatness losses, but the deeper subjective meanings of your movement defy science. Unless you are willing to embrace the ideological extremism of scientism, represented by the phrase, "if you can't measure it, it doesn't exist," you will probably agree that there seems to be more than a trivial relationship between ideas and actions. If you are more than an automaton during your movement experiences, you are straddling the mind/body chasm. It is the quality of this relationship that forms the very essence of many popular activities, particularly in the East, as we will see in a later chapter.

Philosophic skills in action

Philosophy is an avenue down which we can travel to discover the meaning in movement. It imparts a sense of direction to our search and a sense of purpose to the selection and conduct of our activity. The skills of philosophic thinking are eminently adaptable to the movement realm.

Exercise 1-7: Selecting an activity philosophically

If you want to maximize your satisfaction as you select and then participate in physical activity, activate the critical thinking skills of reacting, self-distancing, identifying, analyzing and synthesizing.

Use this table as you conduct a personalized experiment into your own movement choices.

Philosophic Skills	Selection of Activity	Conduct of Activity
Reacting		
Self-Distancing		
Identifying		
Analyzing		

Given that there are only so many hours in the day and that you have a busy lifestyle, how do you decide which recreational activities you will elect to do at any given time? I'm sure that the logistics of your situation are a determining factor. For instance, you can only participate in activities that you can afford, that are available in your area and that you are physically suited for, but even within those limitations there is certainly some room for choice.

Read the following criteria and then use them to analyze two different activities. The first physical activity is one in which you participated prior to encountering these philosophic skills. The second is one in which you participate as soon as possible after reading this discussion. In this you should carefully and deliberately allow these skills to govern your selection and conduct of activity. Record the specifics of your case on the table and examine the qualitative differences between the movement experiences.

Discussion: For philosophy to take place there has to be some form of **reaction**. Asleep, or in a comatose state, you do not react to what is going on around you. As you become more alert, your interest is triggered by a statement, your observations or an issue that occurs to you and you decide to think more deeply about your course of action before proceeding any further. So, reacting is rather like awakening to a situation. Now what might you be reacting to when you choose a physical activity? The mirror perhaps, or the bathroom scales! Perhaps you are awakening to the sad fact that you don't look or feel the way you want to. Perhaps you realize that you are not moving proficiently or efficiently. Is your reaction more health-based (for example, prompted by a history of heart disease in the family, stress at work or a wish to avoid the ailments associated with aging, such as arthritis)? Alternatively, you may be reacting to a ho-hum existence, searching for a little more joy or excitement through a physical experience. Your reaction may be fitness, health or happiness-related, all of the above or none of the above. In retrospect, consider which factors governed your initial reaction to your earlier experience and through thoughtful premeditation, determine what you are reacting to as you pick your next activity. The nature of this awakening will have profound ramifications for the subsequent choice of activity. Just as the punishment should fit the crime, so the action should fit the reaction.

Self-distancing entails taking a step back from the immediate situation to give yourself time and space to reflect in a relatively dispassionate manner. It may be that, although you can appreciate the value of detachment for philosophy, you are not accustomed to treating your recreational moments in like fashion. Many "weekend warriors" leap into their activities feet first with little or no forethought. Such rash actions can have serious, debilitating consequences. If only they would spend one iota of the time and attention they devote to considering the "serious" matters of life, (such as the advisability of investing in a particular mutual fund), to their recreational choices, they would realize how inappropriate some of their selections really are. Look before you leap is a motto that appropriately describes the demeanor that you should adopt in order to distance yourself during the process of activity selection. As you reach this reflective, detached state, consider and record what your initial inclinations were and in what ways they seem inappropriate upon further consideration.

The process of **identification** involves looking inwards at yourself and outwards at your options. It entails introspection to identify your aptitudes and attitudes. A good starting point is your fitness profile. What are you capable of doing? Examine the uniqueness of your own body and its physiology. Most self-inflicted recreational injuries could have been prevented if only the victims had taken the time to identify their own strengths and weaknesses before embarking upon their course of action. A complete personal aptitude inventory extends beyond fitness capacity to include skill level. It is not very rewarding to be completely over your head or to be bored by the lack of challenge in an activity. To avoid such an eventuality, take a few minutes to accurately assess your own skill level. In some activities that is an easier task than in others. In tennis, for example, the United States Tennis Association has established a ranking system to enable such self-assessment. Such guidelines are well intentioned but vague, as tennis players will attest, because they depend upon self-reporting. The variability between 4.5 rated tennis players, for example, is at least partly attributable to the willingness and proficiency of these self-raters to perform the philosophic skill of detached identification.

Having established the parameters of your body's capacities, a second important phase in the process of fitness identification is to determine what type of activity your body most needs. To establish an accurate aptitude profile, a blend of philosophical and physiological information and expertise is necessary whereas to identify attitudes a background in psychology is highly desirable. With the help of tests which have been designed to measure your mood states and your personality traits, it is highly desirable to look inward to determine which needs you wish to satisfy through your activities and then, to choose accordingly. To identify the ideal choice, you must marry your aptitudes and your attitudes with the most appropriate activity available. Once again, the key to your selection is identification. Start by surveying organized recreation in your environment, but don't forget that many of the most satisfying movement experiences can be of your own making. Next, record on your table a list of the characteristics that you observe in yourself after assessing your aptitudes and attitudes. Also make a short list of the activities that you identify as available to you. Look at this list and consider the extent to which your recent movement experiences have been a good match with your own personal profile.

Through the process of identification, which is essentially information gathering, the stage is set for the critical final stages of your movement choice. **Analyzing** demands that you ask yourself some very tough questions, for example,

- given what you know about your physiological profile, what balance do you want to strike between different fitness types and different systems of the body? Perhaps you have tended to emphasize one fitness type, for example strength, over others, such as agility, flexibility, power and endurance, in the past. Similarly, you may have tended to gravitate toward programs of exercise that would benefit your respiratory or your muscular system without really making conscious choices. Has your decision-making been reflexive or reflective to this point? If reflective, you have probably given the makeup and needs of your body serious consideration before selecting an activity. Reflexive decision-making resembles the immature knee-jerk reaction stage of philosophic decision-making: reacting emotionally to a stimulus, flying to conclusions and taking the first easy course of action that presents itself. Here you are presented with the opportunity to move up the scale from reflexivity toward reflectivity along both philosophical and physiological parameters.

- how do you want to prioritize your psychological needs? Perhaps you identified affiliation, recognition, leadership, self-discovery and a sense of worth as the outcomes you particularly seek through movement experiences. If so, the next step is to identify and embark upon a course of action that will meet these needs. The problem that you might find yourself dealing with is that few activities meet all of these needs. The few that might do so will cater to them disproportionately, for example high in recognition and leadership outcomes but low in affiliation potential. Distinguishing how these needs might be met through your choices and deciding which needs to meet first are basic analytical tasks in the choosing process, the results of which you should record on the table provided.

The culmination of this exercise of using philosophic skills to determine your choice of action is the **synthesizing** process. This entails constructing your own best solution by taking a wide-angle lens perspective. You have awakened to the fact that it is in your best interests to choose an activity. You have taken a step back to consider the situation from a distance. You have identified important features in your profile and in the opportunities before you and you have carefully analyzed what is most important to you. Now it only remains to put the icing on the cake. Look as broadly as you can at the array of options that present themselves to you to find the ones that most closely meet your needs. Perhaps you have identified high risk and high endurance as your top priority - how about an outdoor adventure experience, like rock-climbing and rapelling? Alternatively, your preference may be for activities of a more sedentary cerebral nature, in which case check into the tai chi class at the local Y, or the yoga program being offered at the Recreation Center. If the perfect solution to your search doesn't materialize, use your initiative to fabricate your own movement experience. To complete this exercise, record(on the table provided) the recreational activity that you discover most closely meets the criteria you have established and the details of one activity that you would invent to fill those unique specifications.

This personalized experiment was designed to demonstrate how the philosophic process can be adapted to improve your decision-making when selecting activities that will not only fill your time, but also fulfil your needs.

Exercise 1-8: Participating in an activity philosophically

We will now focus on the next phase of what you may have formerly considered to be a physical process: the participatory stage. Underlying both of these narratives is the thesis that the philosophical and the physical elements of being are inextricably interwoven. Even in the heat of the athletic contest, clear and orderly thinking will enhance your effectiveness. Next time you play a sport make a conscious effort to concentrate on the philosophic phases we have discussed. After the event is over, take the time to analyze the effect of this experiment on your game.

As you enter the contest, **react** in a more deliberate fashion than you normally would to the setting, to your opponent's demeanor, to your own feelings and to what you observe your opponent trying to do. For example, if you are playing tennis, **identify** the position of the sun, the strength and direction of the wind, the nature of the court surface and the dimensions of the playing area beyond the court markings. Reacting to the setting will help you to decide how and where you will serve, whether and when to use a lob, if a serve/volley strategy might be effective and whether you have the space to slug it out from behind the baseline. Next, take a good hard look at your opponent's demeanor [without antagonizing by staring!] What do the facial mannerisms suggest - concern, determination, agitation, distraction?

What about your opponents posture? Is this the slumped figure of one who is resigned to defeat before you? React to these cues as you determine your own game strategy. Make mental notes about your own condition - do you feel confident, energetic and poised for victory? Playing within these feelings is the conceptual basis of successful training methods, such as the fartlek approach, and successful strategies in competition. For example, if you hear a marathon winner explaining that she just ran within herself, she probably means that she responded to the fluctuations in her own condition throughout the race. She never pushed herself too hard (to the point of physiological meltdown), but always stayed as close as she could to that upper limit. Finally, react to what your opponent is trying to do, even before the game begins. For example, many a close game of tennis is won or lost during the warm-up. Look carefully at your opponent's game to see how he moves, whether he favors the forehand drive over the backhand, which spin he is using on his drives and which of your spins he is comfortable handling. Look further to see whether he seems awkward at the net, how he transitions from the baseline to the net and whether he seems to have directional control of his serves and a preference for serving to a particular area of your service box.

Self-distancing is often critical to success on the playing field. After identifying your opponent's preferences, a philosophically mature player will step back from the situation to think about how these observed characteristics can be used to construct a winning strategy. From the beginning of the game, an element of detachment is desirable in order to pursue your goal. Disruption through intimidation, violence and trash-talking is a frequently used strategy in contact sports, such as football, basketball, hockey, rugby and soccer which is designed to break down this attempt at self-distancing, to destroy preconceived strategies and to get the other team to be reactive rather than proactive.

Although a passion to play and to win is a prerequisite to sporting success in many instances, it is obviously desirable to maintain a dispassionate demeanor by maintaining an element of detachment in the face of such attempts. The players who are effective self-distancers are more likely to be good coaches than athletes who get so wrapped up in what they are doing that by the conclusion of the contest, they may have won the game but they have no idea why. To coach well, one must have the vision that comes from stepping back, observing the bigger picture and identifying the finer points of the situation. The most essential element of successful playing and coaching is also the ultimate goal of the philosophical thinking process: **analyzing** [your opponent's weaknesses and your strengths] and **synthesizing** [a winning strategy based on this analysis]. At the highest levels of professional and Olympic sports, a veritable army of skilled analysts works to enhance performance and to plot ways to exploit perceived weaknesses in an opponent's arsenal of skills. You may not be a member of that elite cadre but your game may still benefit from the processes of reacting, identifying, self-distancing, analyzing and synthesizing. Try it and if you record any significant differences you will have experienced the benefit of philosophy in action.

Philosophic awareness through action

In the previous section, we considered how philosophy can be used to enhance your athletic prowess. However, the benefits of philosophy extend far beyond the dimension of increasing your movement effectiveness to affect every facet of your being. In the remaining chapters of this book, we will use the philosophic approach we have already developed to examine the very important ways of learning and growing through philosophy.

Without a doubt, the central aim of this search for wisdom is to facilitate **self-understanding**. Unlike many college courses, which are designed to give you knowledge about things around you, philosophy challenges you to carefully consider the thoughts within you. Rather than being expected to absorb the knowledge that is presented to you, you will be asked to reflect on questions that often have no clear-cut answers. Rather than being asked to regurgitate information that you have memorized from books and lectures, you will be asked to think for yourself, often about yourself. This phrase should not be interpreted to suggest that such thinking should take place in a vacuum of information, nor that philosophic thinking is a narcissistic parade of opinions. The way of thinking is rigorous and is likely to challenge cherished premises, to shatter equilibrium and to be quite unsettling to one accustomed to living an unexamined existence. The "texts" that will inform our thinking are the ideas of those who have walked down similar pathways before us. Part of the challenge will be to understand the arguments contained in these texts and to identify which have relevance to our predicaments today. The essential elements of the philosophic process are analysis and synthesis. By probing deeply with incisive questions we will attempt to cut to the core arguments, then by drawing on our knowledge of the bigger picture, we will try to piece together the puzzle of our existence. This process, in itself, will lead to a measure of self-understanding.

The emphasis on the moving being, which is central to kinesiology, provides our field with a topic area that is rich in its potential for self-awareness. Our self-understanding is inevitably tied up with our physical being. The person whom you encounter in the mirror every morning is certainly a body, but what else? Are you essentially three entities [mind, body, soul], as dualists suggest, or are you a unity, a whole person? From this basic premise emanates a whole world-view which affects your attitudes toward yourself and your society. Another basic element of self-understanding to be addressed in some depth in the next chapter is what you can learn about yourself through your movement and how developing somatic awareness is a powerful form of self-discovery. The exercises in this chapter will take the form of self-assessments of both your perceptions of your body-mind relationship and the meanings that you ascribe to your movement experiences. Perhaps you will slip on the shoes of the marathon runner who reported that her running was, "a kind of communion" that stretches far beyond simply staying in shape. For her, it is introspection, insight, vulnerability, self-discovery and even identity, which forms an inexplicable bond of humanity. These are powerful words indeed. Do they describe common insights?

Our world seems to be shrinking. Advances in technology allow us to visit, to call, to interface with almost anyone, anywhere at any time. Information systems and communications capabilities give access to the rest of the world, but they do not, in themselves, help us in **understanding others**. They can all be very useful in educating us about other cultures, but you must be willing to embark upon a metaphorical journey if you are to understand other peoples. We will travel together to foreign lands to discover how cultures steeped in their own traditions view their bodies, their movement and their philosophy in action, perhaps to get a glimpse of your own future. The days of parochialism have passed. Like it or not, you will, in all likelihood, be an active member of the world community in the twenty-first century. As such, you will need to overcome ethnocentrism in your own perspective and in the attitudes of others. As far as possible, you should learn to walk in their shoes and to see the world through their eyes if you are to interact effectively with people from other cultures. From a more selfish perspective, when you encounter world-views that are not congruent with your own, but which seem to work for others, you tend to reassess your own perspectives, leading to philosophic growth. For example, exposure to the power of the chi and the meridians of the body will probably galvanize you to reexamine your attitudes toward your own moving body and it's anatomy. This chapter is designed to leave you with the big picture of philosophy, a global perspective that weaves together the west and the east. The exercises challenge you to assess, modify and, perhaps, reaffirm your philosophy on issues of universal importance.

Philosophy will help you to appreciate various aspects of your being more fully and to experience them more richly. Aesthetic dimensions of your being, such as **playing** and **appreciating the beauty in movement** contribute to the goal of living **the good life.** Playing is within the purview of kinesiology, but more important, it is essential to your quality of life. Typically, society tends to dismiss the need for thoughts on play with such phrases as, "just do it." After all, children seem to have no trouble playing, so why should more mature beings require guidance? Such skeptics fail to see that the socialization process, that all adults have been subject to, involves unlearning play. It would not be seemly for a mature person to act spontaneously in displays of unfettered exuberance. Future colleagues will look askance at you if you suddenly decide to roll in the newly mown grass outside your office just because it smells good, you feel like it and it is there. Growing up entails developing a veneer of sophistication that hardens you to such impulses. You learn through repeated behavioral reinforcement at home, in school and at work to suppress, repress and even to exterminate those childlike impulses. For example, the desire to dance and sing when you are happy, to cry and hug when you feel sad and to express yourself openly, unassumingly and physically whenever you feel like it. Philosophy can have an important role in reinstating play into your lives. The first aspect of this process, which we will consider in the chapter on playing, is the scope of the phenomenon of play. Through metaphysical analysis, we can attempt to define play, both in abstract universal terms and in an immediate personal way that will have relevance to your daily life. Because philosophy is someone else's philosophy until you experience it, you will be encouraged through assigned exercises to seek to appreciate the importance of play in your life by learning through doing. From these rudimentary beginnings, you will be asked to react to your play experiences in various ways, to step back from the process to identify core components and common denominators in your play choices. Finally, and most important, you will analyze your own play patterns and consider alternatives in order to synthesize a truly satisfying pathway to play for yourself.

Throughout the kinesiology curriculum, you are taught to understand human movement but where is appreciating movement emphasized? At one level you may appreciate the interrelated complexity of the body, the efficiency of the human organism and the satisfaction of enhancing performance through science and technology. Yet, this is more a vicarious, detached, qualitative, response than the personal reaction that you have to the thrill of victory and the agony of defeat. It embraces such experiences as the feelings of the warm wind caressing your face as you horse ride or the sights as you jog along the cliff top in the summer sunset. Perhaps, experiences such as these attracted you to the study of human movement in the first place. If so, it may have disappointed you to discover how dissociated the scholarly study of movement can be from the experience itself. Instead of being the source of your laughter, joy and achievement, the body is often treated like a machine. Its parts are probed and dissected, its functions are examined and enhanced and its interactions are hypothesized and measured. Although such scientific exploration may seem to be a far cry from the lived moment, there is one branch of kinesiology that does ask you to focus on the quality of your movement experience. Philosophy, and in particular aesthetics, is a lens into the soul of the activity. Appreciation of such facets of your movement as beauty and joy, which the sciences don't touch, is what distinguishes kinesiology as the holistic study of humans moving from the mechanistic study of human movement. As part of the learning process in this chapter you will be asked to discern beauty in your own movement from the dual perspectives of spectator and participant. The ensuing discussion is intended to enhance your aesthetic appreciation, so we will conclude the chapter by testing the extent to which that intention has become reality in your case.

In today's society, **making moral choices** is not an option. The complexity, commercialism and competitiveness of everyday life present you with opportunity after opportunity to choose between right and wrong, or perhaps two alternative rights, or even two wrongs [as in the lesser of two evils]. Because the basis on which you make your choice is an option, ethical analysis is a critical component of your kinesiology curriculum to prepare you for a lifetime of effective decision making. The choices you make determine whether you will **take the right path through life**. In every sphere of life intimately related to kinesiology, ethics is crucial. Sport is ethics in action. Even in the cauldron of competition, you are asked to make split second decisions about cheating and fair play, sportsmanship and gamesmanship. If you are contemplating entering a health-related profession, exercise science or research and development, medical ethics is a background of critical importance to your future. As medical and biotechnological options grow, so do the ethical dilemmas associated with them. In schools, ethical issues are rife. As a teacher, you will be faced with many ethical quandaries brought to you by students relying upon your judgement and wisdom. Wherever you turn, in both your private and your public life, you will be faced with ethical decisions that will affect the quality of your relationships, your conduct and your peace of mind. In the chapter devoted to this topic, you will be presented with various ethical predicaments and asked how you would react. Then, we will distance ourselves from the immediate issue in order to identify the basic moral issues that are woven into this particular problem. Finally, you will analyze a range of approaches to the ethical decision making process to determine which works for you in this particular situation, before synthesizing your own new and improved solution. The payoff is the satisfaction of taking charge of your own life. An unexamined life can seem out of control. Unexpected events broadside you. Your life seems to take a course of its' own. It may even seem to be pointless, meaningless. Without the rudder of philosophy, you may seem to drift aimlessly on the sea of life. In this chapter, you will learn to steer a steady course, even through the squalls of your everyday problems. The exercises you will encounter are designed to help you to distance yourself from the imminent crises and catastrophes that loom large enough in your day to eclipse the horizon and the solutions that you may discover in the distance. You will be encouraged to take a broad view of your life, to develop hindsight so that you may learn from your past and the prescience necessary to analyze your present. From a structured process of identification of trends in your life and interpolation of your interests and needs, you will synthesize a strategy for the conduct of your life that should help you when you encounter the vicissitudes and the opportunities of your existence.

Review

In this introduction you have encountered and experienced the philosophic process. You have learned that philosophy is the search for wisdom and you have embarked on a personal quest through a series of exercises. In the process, you have probably realized that becoming more philosophical is in your best interests for a number of reasons. The physical and the philosophical, which may have seemed remotely related at the outset, are intricately intertwined in reality, as the examination of philosophy in action indicated. The study of philosophy in kinesiology is not a luxury, but an imperative if you are concerned about self-awareness and the quality of the movement experience. To check your own understanding, you might want to respond to the following questions:

1. In what ways is philosophy inactive, in what ways active?

2. Why is reacting an important first step in the philosophic process?

3. Self-distancing is desirable, but impossible. What are the limits of your objectivity?

4. How can the process of identification help you to plan your next work out?

5. Analyzing is a critical process. Does that mean that it is entirely negative in nature?

6. Why is synthesizing described as the soul of the philosophic process?

7. How does the meaning you find in movement transcend the physical domain?

Part II

DEVELOPING UNDERSTANDING

Chapter 2
SELF-UNDERSTANDING

Preview

In this chapter, you will examine the following aspects of self-understanding:

- Meanings of "self"
- Forms that "understanding" may take
- Ways of understanding your self
- Meaning in your movement experiences
- The importance of self-understanding

Understanding Self-Understanding

A Sense of Self

The study of the derivation of words provides fascinating insights into the affairs and times of bygone generations. Have you considered the derivation of your own name? Many words that are in popular usage today have lost their original connotation, for instance, a "gymnasium" is no longer a place where nude athletes congregate. Another word that leads us into the topic of this chapter is selfish. The word's linguistic roots reflects the perturbation of a culture trying to come to terms with an amorphous concept. "Ish" generally means "an approximation of" in general usage, as in "brownish" or "softish." Because the concept of self is so difficult to define in a clear and acceptable manner, former generations may well have coined the term self "ish" to give them some leeway. To broach the tricky topic of understanding self, here is an exercise designed to help you assess where you are now, which we can call your Self "ish" Self-Study.

Exercise 2-1: Selfish Self-Study

Place yourself on the spectrum between each of the paired statements below by circling the number that identifies your philosophic position:

1. You are body, mind, soul   1   2   3   (4) 5   You cannot be divided into discrete parts

2. Education is for the life of the mind   1   2   3   (4) 5   Education is for the whole being

3. PE is for a sound mind in a healthy body   1   2   3   (4) 5   PE is for well being

4. You have a body   1   (2) 3   4   5   You are a body

5. Basketball free throw shooting is largely mental   1   2   3   (4) 5   is concentrated effort

18

Discussion: To the extent that language is descriptive, you have displayed the degree of dualism with which you regard your self. If your score is low [5-10], you tend to view your body and mind as separate and distinct entities. A high score [20-25] signifies that you see your self as a unified whole. As we will see later in this chapter, perspectives on this topic vary widely, but there is unanimity that the way you see yourself will affect the way you interact with your world.

Now, as you proceed along your philosophic journey, you will pass from the realm of metaphysical speculation, where you have been conducting an ontological examination of the nature of being, to an epistemological consideration of how we know.

Understanding Understanding

Understanding entails gathering and integrating information through the processes of experience and reflection. Information gathering takes place constantly through our senses. In everything you do, you are aware of the sights, sounds, smells, taste and feel of your surroundings. As you move, your kinesthetic sense organs provide further sensory input. Through these senses you learn to understand your world. Try the following experiment to verify how important your senses are to your comprehension and competence.

Exercise 2-2: How do we know?

Sensory understanding

Deprive yourself systematically of your sight, hearing, and touch as you conduct a series of everyday activities, for example taking a nature walk, playing a game of your choice and preparing a meal. Work with a partner as you use sensory deprivation techniques, such as wearing blindfolds, earplugs and thick latex gloves.

Discussion: Through these exercises, you will become aware of your dependence on your senses, most notably sight, and of the challenges that are faced on a daily basis by the blind and the deaf.

Empirical data gathering is not only the basis of what you know personally, it is also the basis of what we know as a culture through scientific research. The experimental method is founded on the acquisition and manipulation of observed data.

Even though this information enters your consciousness, it must be assimilated into your world-view before it can be considered to be your understanding. What you know to be your perception and what you understand to be your reality might be quite different. A purpose and function of the philosophic process is to help you to make personally acceptable sense of what may otherwise be a random and disconnected collection of observations. This integration process takes the form of disciplined thinking.

Scientific understanding

To help you to cultivate your reasoning powers, try the following partner exercise.

Select a research conclusion in our field, concerning such topics as the benefits or dangers of exercise, obesity or alcohol use, and try to find weaknesses in the experimental design and false premises on which conclusions were founded.

Discussion: As you become more proficient at establishing the legitimacy of truth claims, you are taking an important first step on the path to understanding by developing **healthy skepticism**.

Exercise 2-3: Questioning and defining

Healthy skepticism

Take a frequently used conclusion from your interest area [for example, sports build character], identify the key words and carefully define them. With a partner compare definitions to see what other ways there are of understanding words and concepts. Distinguish common ground with your partner so that you may rework your definitions to be mutually agreeable.

Discussion: In this stage of the exercise, you have been developing **definitional dexterity**.

Definitional dexterity

Pick an issue that is hotly disputed today, for example whether affirmative action is desirable in college sports. Examine it, not from the perspective of the answer, but by asking what fundamental questions does it raise? As you do so, try to distinguish the central problem from the various side issues.

Discussion: You are now engaging in a form of philosophic exercise as a means of pursuing truth and understanding that dates back through the centuries to the original Socratic dialogues: clarification through **questioning** ever deeper and deeper.

Exercise 2-4: Logical reasoning

Inductive reasoning

Play "Sherlock". In other words, assume the role of a detective (such as Sherlock Holmes) with an issue, such as how to construct the perfect diet. Identify the various components of the puzzle and then construct the perfect solution by pulling all the parts of the problem together.

Discussion: The logical process you have just engaged in is **inductive reasoning**.

Deductive reasoning

Take a concept and extract it's particular characteristics. To help you in this exercise, let's take the example of sport. Perhaps you would say that its features include a level of physical exertion and competitiveness. You can then logically deduce the sporting nature of any activity because it is physically demanding and competitive. As new evidence is introduced to your equation, you will alter your definition accordingly. If, for example, evidence is compelling that chess is a sport, you will re-assess your criteria. You may decide that cerebral activity or very fine motor skills are adequate: so chess is a sport, or you may reject chess on the basis that it is not physically demanding. The logical process is flexible to the extent that conclusions are constantly re-evaluated as new information comes to light. Now conduct this exercise with a concept of your own choice.

Discussion: This is a process of **deduction**, in which you have moved from the general concept to the specific components. _end → beginning_

These forms of reasoning are the building blocks to clearer understanding. They are also a means by which you can develop greater self-understanding in repose and in recreation. Learning and understandings do not just transpire in the classroom, or through bookish study. They take place in every walk of life. Generally speaking, the more you are engaged in, and by, an experience, the more likely it is to stimulate meaningful learning. Think of your own biography. Have your movement experiences been memorable, even inspirational, on occasions? If so, it is likely that they have contributed in profound ways to your self-understanding.
→ taught me: lax = non-aggressive, non-competitive; laying on the ocean = enjoying nature around me

Self-Understanding Through Movement

Self-Mastery

You have probably found unique forms of self-understanding in, and through, your movement experiences. The cerebral skills that are essential elements of becoming more philosophical and of developing your reasoning powers are integral to the movement process in that you must make choices as you develop strategies and reason carefully even as you move artfully. The movement experience is a unique setting for philosophic growth. Only in this context do you learn as you project yourself through space, often with vigorous intensity. The first lesson you learn on the path to self-understanding is **self-mastery**.

Moving leads to removing. The frustrations of the everyday world slip away as you play, run, sweat and laugh. You have found a medium of which you can be master. Although you may still struggle with your own limitations, you want to be there, you have hope of improving and you enjoy the challenge. Thwarted in a particular task, you draw on the sensory input of the occasion to figure out what went wrong. Perhaps you were trying to master a topspin backhand in a tennis match but couldn't seem to stop the ball from burying itself in the net. The sensory input from what you saw and felt in your own action combined with data from such secondary sources as videotapes and the observations of coaches [if you are fortunate enough to have access to them] are the basis for rectifying the problem. Having the information is not, in itself, a guarantee of mastery. Perfecting a skill, such as that backhand, entails using other skills with dexterity: the philosophical skills of analysis and synthesis. Like a doctor, you must correctly identify the symptoms and then prescribe the best cure. Some backhands are so riddled with "dis-ease" that the highest level of analysis is necessary to distinguish all the ailments, to differentiate between their relative severity and to determine which should be treated first. Synthesizing a remedy is equally problematic. Should you attend to footwork first or is the grip the first order of importance, or perhaps the swing?

Mastery extends beyond skill acquisition to encompass all aspects of the activity, including techniques and tactics, equipment use and maintenance, preparation and participation. Perhaps even more important is the mastery of self. In the "heat of battle" you can experience the gamut of emotions: joy and sadness, exuberance and exhilaration, frustration and anger. Learning how to deal with and express these feelings is part and parcel of learning to play the game and learning to understand yourself. To experience such self-mastery, perform the following exercises and consider the results.

Exercise 2-5: Acquiring skills philosophically

Mastering skill acquisition

Select a skill that you want to learn but that you have difficulty performing. Try it, and record the problems you have with it. Now, carefully analyze the information you collected to determine the relative severity of the glitches and where the break-down seems to start. Identify the core problem and synthesize a strategy for success. Implement it and ask did it work? If not, go back to the drawing board and develop a new blueprint until you hit one that is effective

Mastering skills cooperatively

Repeat the process with a partner, this time acting as "coach." Be your partner's eyes and ears to gather data and then go through the process of analysis and synthesis with your protégé.

Developing self-mastery

As you play your favorite activity, be conscious of the feelings you go through. While the experience is still fresh in your mind, record the emotions you mastered. Reflect back to earlier experiences and think about your emotions in the following ways:

- those you have most trouble expressing,

- those that you can't seem to suppress,

- those that you are able to channel positively

- and those that end up hurting your performance.

What conclusions do you draw about changes in your own self-mastery through movement experiences?

Self-Discovery

Even as you encounter your own shortcomings and your own fears, you are learning to understand what you want to do, what you can do and what your limits are. The movement experience is an avenue to **self-discovery**. Selection of movement preferences is a marriage. You look for a partner who is like you, who complements you, who you find agreeable. So, choosing well depends upon your self-knowledge and your ability to identify components in a game or activity that are compatible with your nature. You don't want a partner that is aggressive, angry and even hostile [as boxing and football can be], if you yearn for the peaceful, tranquil life [maybe hiking or bowling]. Activities have characters just like people. Part of the process of self-discovery is selecting and sampling a range of movement experiences to find out just who you are. An interesting exercise involves fleshing out the personality of an activity.

Exercise 2-6: Play and personality

Identifying the personality of play

dancing
→aerobic
→art
→not-competitive

Pick a pastime near and dear to your heart and inductively create an individual from the qualities you perceive it to have. These personal qualities include

- personality type [calm or exciting, cautious or risky, conservative or audacious, gentle or aggressive, loud or quiet and so on], *not-aggressive, loud, fun, spontaneous*
- physical mannerisms [for example, strong, powerful, agile, flexible, quick, deliberate, sustained, explosive], *deliberate, beautiful, flexible, difficult*
- location [indoors, outdoors, gym, playing field, track, pool, lake, rivers, beaches, mountains, foreign country etc.]. *anywhere! → that's what's great about it.*

With a little imagination, you should be able to construct a plausible person out of such criteria, even to the point of giving him/her a name.

Picking a personality

Now deduce from knowledge of your desires and needs, which sport or pastime would ideally suit you [for the purposes of this exercise, ignore the logistics of availability, cost, etc. - just focus on the perfect mate!] *dancing*

As much as self-understanding may derive from activity selection, it is in the participatory stages that you learn most about yourself. Involvement in physical activity brings you face to face with yourself. The medium of movement is uniquely capable of confronting you with your own human frailty. Your hopes and fears are realized. You are on display in a public arena where your mode of expression is overtly physical. Private experience of your limitations becomes a public expression of humbling proportions. In most spheres of life, you can hide your failings and failures. In the realm of the body, there is no place to hide. Every part of your physical being is right there for participants and observers to see. Play becomes display. In a very public arena, you learn what you can and cannot do. Try as you might, some moves are beyond your capacity. There are limits to your performance. Your physiological makeup prescribes your actions. Your psychological profile inscribes your reactions. Movement is a medium that will test and prove your limits. It is also a pathway to your potential. It can help you to understand what you cannot do, but it also holds the promise of what you can do. It is a gauge against which you can measure improvement. It is a constant in an uncertain world of change. As you age, it provides a way of expressing youthful impulses, of pushing back time. It is a rock that you can hang onto as time rushes by. It is a pool into which you can dive to discover the treasures of your existence hidden deep below the surface. It is the mountain top that lures you upward to discover your potential. Physical activity is much more than a physiological workout. It is an opportunity for you to experience yourself in new and different ways, to understand yourself more fully and to strive for the ultimate state of self- awareness in which you achieve unity in yourself and harmony with your surroundings.

Body of Knowledge

Philosophy of the body

The way you view the body in relation to your mind is the way you view yourself. The Selfish Self-Study that you completed at the beginning of this chapter gave you some idea of your own self-perception. If you compare notes with others, you will probably find a high level of variability among your peers. Similarly, attitudes on this issue have fluctuated widely from culture to culture through the ages. Eastern societies, especially those with Buddhist and Taoist leanings, have taken a more unified approach to human being than western culture in the last two thousand years. Whereas the East considers the self to be the physical functioning of the mind, the western approach has been to separate the mind and the body into two discrete units. Our earliest ancestors cared little for such distinctions, for they inhabited a world in which they were immersed in the raw experience provided by the structure and functioning of the body itself. It was the later Greek epoch that gave birth to the concept of mind as an intangible complement to the temporal body. It also established a hierarchy: the mind became the captain of the body vessel. The religion of the Middle Ages further compounded the division between mind and body by decreeing that since the soul was eternal and the body mortal, salvation would come through spiritual cultivation. The body should be healthy to uphold the sanctity of the spirit, but should otherwise be controlled, disciplined and ignored until it passed away. During the Renaissance period, the humanism of the age gave a new respect for the body. It became an aspect of a person worthy of cultivation, as a vehicle for creative expression and for living fully in the here and now.

This recognition of the value of physical being and partial integration of the body into the self came to an abrupt halt in the seventeenth century due to the extraordinary influence of the ideas of one man. Rene Descartes' famous dictum, "I think. Therefore, I am," signaled the beginning of an era of dualism that has dominated the philosophic landscape ever since. He saw mind and body as separate and distinct entities, each with its own characteristics. The mind is the unextended, immaterial substance that does the thinking. In contrast, the body is a figure bounded by time and space that is divisible and non-thinking. The mind and the body are so mutually exclusive, according to Cartesian dualism, that people virtually live at two parallel, but disconnected, levels. In the process of proving his own existence, Descartes rejected the evidence from the body, because he doubted the accuracy of sensory perceptions, favoring instead the proof supplied by his mind in the form of his rational thought processes. Descartes was a preeminent proponent of the philosophic technique of skepticism. His methodology of "radical doubt" produced the doctrine of "clear and distinct ideas."

Subsequently, thinking and moving have rarely been equated. Thinking has assumed a preeminent status in western society and moving has been relegated to a secondary level of importance. Consequently, education sees it's primary mission as enhancing the life of the mind. Physical activity is extra-curricular, something to do at recess or to recreate [so that students may once again be ready to get down to the serious business of study]. In such an atmosphere, education of and through the physical does not get much respect or room in the curriculum. Other philosophic explanations of the self have been proposed, but none have supplanted the Cartesian position in western culture that we are composed of two separate entities: mind and body.

Berkeley suggested that we are mind only and that our being is in our perception. Theories of physicalism, or materialism, which explain self as body only have not won a wide following because of their limited explanatory power, but have gained some credibility from research showing that emotional response is attributable, in part, to the secretion of hormones and chemical processes in the body.

More pervasive in its influence than physicalism, existential phenomenology has developed the notion of embodied consciousness to explain the concept of self. Maurice Merleau-Ponty was one representative of this school of thought who rejected the Cartesian mind-body split and the implicit assumption that the body was an object to be acted upon. Rather, phenomenologists suggest, the body is the starting point of our lives, the means by which we insert ourselves into our world, a "lived-body." It is not an object to be manipulated by our minds, but a subject through which we live, through which we act upon others and through which we develop dialectical relationships with the world around us.

Science of the body

Science and philosophy are not strangers or enemies. In fact, they are often bosom buddies, mutually involved in advancing knowledge. Science is premised on philosophy. If you try to conduct an experiment in which you have no premises about what science is or what it can do, no purpose beyond the mechanics of testing, no logic, no ethics and no principles, it will probably not be well-received. Similarly, philosophy is premised on science, often as a starting point for reflection. Asking questions such as "what if?", "how do we know?" and "what do we mean by?" philosophers extend the boundaries of science by venturing into territory forbidden to science, where there are no tests to measure validity, no definite answers, only questions.

The ventures of science and philosophy are not separate and distinct. They are symbiotically linked, often embodied into one great thinker. History is replete with examples of such individuals who have transcended one paradigm of thought. Galileo, Copernicus, DaVinci, Newton and Einstein are examples of a genre of thinkers who would not allow themselves to be limited in their approach to a problem of their times. At the frontiers of science today, there are new perspectives and scientific evidence for the interconnectedness between consciousness and the material world that suggest that self is an integrated, unified entity. Questions about the self tend to be avoided by modern science and passed on to the philosophers. Examples of such profound questions are what is mind? what is the nature of matter? and, how are they related?

Most scientists today adopt the western perspective that an objective reality exists external to us and independent of our minds. Our role, then, is to observe and measure what we see, but as a passenger not a participant. However, the notion of separability between consciousness and matter within science is being challenged by certain interpretations of quantum theory and by ancient eastern theory. These apparently divergent approaches converge in their contention that the observer interacts fundamentally with the system in the act of observation. The scientific paradigm based upon the powers of the eye and the mind (empirical observation and data-gathering followed by rigorous logical data analysis), is being supplanted by knowledge grounded in the experience of lived-body. The traditional approach that gives legitimacy only to what science could observe, measure and explain is shifting to incorporate the more interior worlds of consciousness and spirit. We are in the midst of a paradigm shift away from the old Cartesian, Newtonian mechanistic paradigm to a new paradigm which is the holistic, ecological world view.

Such thinking represents a fundamental challenge to the way we do science in kinesiology. We are in the body business. In an anatomy lab, we probe it to understand its structure and we "read" it as the course text. In physiology, we subject it to stress tests to ascertain the limits of its functioning. In a motor learning course, we examine skill acquisition, transfer of training and retention as constructs that are generalizable to populations of motor learners. In a motor control experiment, we study epiphenomenon of the brain resulting from complex biophysical processes. In a biomechanics class, we do engineering of the body. In each case, we tend to treat the body as an object to be studied much as geologists study a rock. It is interesting to speculate how, as kinesiology adopts the new insights into the properties of consciousness and the interconnection between consciousness and matter into its operational framework, the way we do the body business will be affected.

Living Through The Body

Being

To an extent, your being is determined by your seeing. The way you see yourself affects the way you act, the things you do, the people you hang around with, in short, everything about you. This process of seeing yourself cannot be of a sensory nature because we do not have eyes that turn inward. It is rather a process of self-perception that is colored less by our vision than by our attitudes and beliefs. Together, these attitudes and beliefs constitute your world- view, which is the primary determinant of who you are.

This world-view is not static, except in the most intransigent of individuals. In most cases, you are in a constant process of changing. The more open you are to the philosophic processes described in this book, the more likely you are to question and attempt to improve your world view. One of the influences you must contend with as you analyze and synthesize your own philosophy is the power of prevailing ideologies. These may take the form of generally accepted codes of thought and of conduct among the group of people you interact with most frequently. For example, if you were to belong to a pack of destitute children roaming the streets of Rio de Janeiro you might expect to have a widely convergent ethical code concerning theft than that adopted by society at large.

Some cultural world views transcend your particular social grouping to form dominant paradigms, such as the scientific paradigm of mechanical reductionism, which includes the Cartesian mind-body split. The impact of this ideology is profound. It causes a condition that is a symptom of the age of scientism, known as ontological schizophrenia. In essence, this means that you see yourself as consisting of several mutually exclusive aspects, not as a whole being. It is a form of an internal disjunction. Many live by this split. For example, it can be reflected in a mechanistic way of thinking about causality as a sequence of physical events in science or life. It manifests itself through a state of disconnectedness. You may feel disengaged from others and from nature. You may even feel estranged from your own physical body. The alternative is to embrace your own somatic self, to live through your body, to become attuned to the discourse of your physical being, to make yourself at home in your own structure.

Exercise 2-7: Dualism

Personal dualism

Discuss the following questions in order to assess the nature of your being:

- Can you more accurately claim that you have a body or that you are a body?

- What difference would it make to your attitudes if you were to adopt the other position?

- How does your dualist/nondualist philosophy affect the way you conduct yourself in sports?

- How would it affect your behavior in an athletic event if you adopted the other position?

Becoming

Being is the origin of your becoming. From this starting point you embark upon your life's journey. What you will become is related to your philosophic growth. This process of maturation includes the extent to which you can question your assumptions and your ability to effect change in the premises that are the basis of your attitudes and behavior. If a dualistic schism is the basis of your philosophy, you may treat your body as an object. Typically, when the body is separated from the self it becomes a problem in need of control or redesigning. It is experienced as a manipulable object that should be molded so that it can fulfill culturally defined expectations. In today's image-conscious society that often means women want to get smaller [slimmer] and men bigger [more muscular]. Seeing the body as manipulable has resulted in an epidemic of anxiety about its shape. The growing incidence of anorexia nervosa, bulimia and steroid use are a testimony to the dualistic notion that we own our bodies, that they are a resource for our use and that we can shape and mold this object to suit our needs.

Through such excesses, the social problem of the body as object may be reaching crisis proportions today. The body has become an object of consumption for the consumer industry, which is the dominant machinery of the capitalist culture of today. One current emphasis is on the fashionable body purchased with the products of the beauty and physical fitness industries. Another focus is longevity. In its efforts to eternally sip from the fountain of youth, western culture has launched a wholesale assault on the body. One facet of the graying of America is the abandon with which many maturing citizens pump their bodies full of chemical additives, vitamin supplements and painkillers to better enjoy the good life.

If you are being and becoming in America, you have no option but to get involved in the controversy. You will either be immersed by a dualistic philosophy of the body and mind or confront the issue and construct an alternative philosophy of self. Developing an alternative is fraught with problems. It is not easy to stand out against a crowd. All around you, people are separating themselves into segments, the thinking part (which is generally highly cherished and well-hidden from public view) and the physical being (which is highly visible, can be reshaped for greater appeal and can be used for pleasurable purposes). In conjunction with others of like philosophy, bodies can be used for mutual gratification in a user society. Developing an alternative in such a milieu takes determination. Since your body is your way of inserting yourself into your world, it is immediately apparent. Your philosophy, however, is not. Consequently, you must convince others that your convictions are different from theirs by word and deed.

Unfortunately, this culture is bereft of words that you could use. Our language is steeped in dualism. It separates into polar opposites. The words we use tend to tease reality apart and project "thingness" at the expense of wholeness. We communicate, and thus understand reality, in terms of dichotomies. Mind and body, self and other, work and play, female and male are examples of the way we see the world in mutually exclusive, hierarchically organized, polar opposites. The ways we speak focus and limit the ways we understand. The quality of being-at-one is essentially ineffable in our culture. Our vocabulary cannot be explicit in describing what such awkward phrases as lived-body, body-subject and embodied experience might mean.

However, difficulty in communicating your philosophy to others should not prevent you from developing an internal discourse. You can develop somatic awareness through listening to yourself to become aware of the vocabulary and rhythms of your physical being without recourse to language. Similarly, you can learn to value your physical being as yourself, to read that self and even to communicate meanings, through the medium of movement when words will not suffice.

Try the following experiments to better understand dualism and its alternative.

Exercise 2-8: Dualism in everyday communication

Dualism on TV

In an evening of television viewing, notice the following:

- which kinds of bodies are glorified

- whether the body is represented as a person or as a thing

- how many examples of dualistic language you can discover.

[Don't forget the commercials]

Language and dualism

Try to describe a recent athletic event to a friend without using any dualistic concepts or terminology.

Exercise 2-9: Holism

Becoming holistic

Spend some quiet time alone getting to know yourself better. Start by focusing on your steady rhythmic breathing and then develop an internal discourse. As you become more adept at looking inward to your inner rhythms, try to engage this mental state as you go about your everyday activities. After doing so, record and discuss the difference this mental state made to the conduct of these activities.

Moving

Actions speak louder than words, as they say. Through your actions you express your feelings, your inner meanings and your philosophy. You also display degrees of dualism. Human action is a means of personal expression, or it can be acting, a form of role-playing. You are role-playing if you view your body as one step removed from your essence, for then you have a separation between intent and action. In that case, "you" view your body as something to be manipulated. "You" decide how it will be used in a particular endeavor. Let's take sport for example.

Exercise 2-10: Degrees of dualism

Why play?

Respond to the following questions. Why do you choose to play a sport? Is it the opportunity to express yourself, to seek pleasure in the joy of the moment and to be one with your surroundings that draws you to the playing field? Or is your motivation extrinsic to the activity itself? Perhaps you are a varsity athlete on scholarship, so you feel obliged to be at practice. Perhaps you want to create the sculpted physique that is bound to enhance your social life. Do you do it to find friends, to get fit, for the thrill of it, to avoid boredom?

If you are an elite athlete, you are probably motivated by the quest for that elusive record performance. Paradoxically, it is at this pinnacle of movement perfection that participants tend to be most dualistic. Top athletes often view their bodies as machines. Like any finely tuned machine, it must be managed, maintained, conditioned and fueled. In some cases, a drop or two of a special performance-enhancement mixture may be blended with the fuel to squeeze a little more productivity from the body-machine. Like any machine, the body is subject to an occasional breakdown. Unlike the bobsledder, the athlete cannot jump into another vehicle for the next run. Sometimes a pit stop is inevitable, but with the help of medical technicians, the athlete is returned to the race as quickly as possible. Millions of research dollars are spent on speeding up the treatment and recovery phases of athletic injuries so that battered and bruised bodies may reenter the fray without a moment's delay. In such cases, bodies are often divorced from their owners, even though they may be willing to "put their bodies on the line" for the chance of winning the big game or breaking a record performance.

The mind/body schism is certainly found in competitive sport, but it affects all realms of movement. In social settings, dualists may try to use their bodies to gain an advantage or may be oblivious to their physical functioning. Because they are not at one with their bodies, they are unaware of internal dialogue and unable to decipher even the loudest cries for help. Lifestyle diseases abound in a society of individuals who have lost touch with their physical being, who don't understand that every movement contains a message and that, in a very real sense, they are their bodies. The alternative is to embrace the experience of the embodied self. This entails regaining control of your movement agenda and determining when, where and under what circumstances you will participate in sport. During the activity, listen carefully to what your body is telling you and respond in a timely fashion to its cues. In all spheres of movement, try to become more physically literate. Learn to decipher somatic messages and to express your deepest insights and passions in an authentic way through your physical being.

To illustrate how your philosophy of dualism influences how you live through the moving body, try this experiment:

How to play with degrees of dualism

Participate in the same sporting event in two quite different ways. In one case, separate yourself [philosophy speaking] from your own body. Treat it as a machine. Talk of it and think of it as though it were an object. In the other case, be your body. Be less concerned with your strategy and execution than your inner rhythm. For example, if you decide to play tennis, play one set with a sole focus on technique. Analyze in excruciating detail how you are gripping the racket, the angle and velocity of your swing and the positioning of your feet. In other words, think about what you must do with your body in order to win. In the second set, concentrate on your inner game. Focus on your breathing. Let the game flow from deep within you. Don't force the outcome, just let it happen.

Review and Preview

In the first section of this chapter, we have examined ways in which movement can contribute to self-understanding. Particularly significant in this respect is the role of the mind/ body relationship. Through the exercises and discussion, you have been challenged to introspectively consider the level of dualism in your own philosophy. The focus of the chapter now shifts to careers. Your future in the field and your philosophy of mind and body are symbiotic. The way you approach your future and the way you understand yourself and others is inextricably intertwined. In this section we will follow the thread of dualism through vocations that are most popular with kinesiology concentrators to see how that philosophy affects the purpose and performance of the practitioner.

Earning a Living Through The Body

Kinesiology graduates are particularly well suited to enter professions that have as their central focus the human body. They are knowledgeable about its structure and function and about the social and psychological processes that surround the movement phenomenon. Consequently, they naturally gravitate toward vocations that focus on enhancing the movement of others, such as in the school system, in sports, in the colleges and in the realm of medicine. Mind/body philosophy is evident and active in each of these career fields. If you are leaning toward teaching, coaching, healing or researching as a way to spend your future, look before you leap. Just as the unexamined life is not worth living, so the unexamined career may not be worth having. This section is designed to help you reflect on the salience of mind/body philosophy as a significant factor in your career choice.

Exercise 2-11: Professional practice and dualism

Select the profession that interests you most and complete the exercise associated with it. It may be that you are contemplating a career as a teacher, a coach or a healer. If so, this exercise will help you to think through how you should approach your professional future.

Teaching with degrees of dualism

At which school do you choose to teach?

Congratulations! Having completed a teacher education program you have received two offers of employment. Both of the elementary schools are well situated for you, the salaries are comparable, but you really don't know which one to choose. To solve the quandary, you decide to pay them both a visit. Upon your arrival, in each case you are ushered into well-appointed gyms staffed by highly trained teachers, but you find the programs to be quite different. In the first, you are impressed by the discipline that you witness as students line up obediently and answer by number. On the day of your visit, class is preparing for the upcoming annual fitness test when the students get to perform as many pull-ups, pushups and sit-ups as they can in a given time. The teacher stands in the middle of the classroom, carefully watching her charges, and occasionally barking out orders or exhorting greater effort. She explains to you that the entire curriculum is geared toward reaching certain fitness goals. She adds that the establishment of national standards has given the Pysical Education program legitimacy in the eyes of the School Board, because they can compare these fitness performances with other schools. She feels much more comfortable with this type of accountability, than with what she considers to be the very nebulous, "woolly', standards of the other school you are going to visit that day. She expresses a certain pride in the fact that all her students are striving for the same goal. She hopes that the new high-tech fitness equipment the school has just bought will increase the efficiency of class periods and the performance of her students, so that Cartesian Elementary School might rise in the school district rankings. As you are about to leave, a discipline problem arises. Apparently, one overweight child has complained that he doesn't enjoy trying to pull his chin up over a bar, partly because he can't do it and partly because all the other kids laugh at him when he tries. The student is punished for his temerity by being made to run around the gym several times as the rest of the class snickers at him.

Down the road at Embodiment Elementary, you encounter a quite different scene. In fact, it is so different that your first inclination is to turn around and walk right back out through the door. In the place of the orderly, silent rows of children intently and seriously working on their fitness tasks, is what seems to be organized mayhem. Children are running around the gym, sometimes talking, often laughing, all apparently doing their own thing. The teacher is too busy to talk to you, because she is flitting from student to student, asking them how their exploration process is going, suggesting alternative solutions and encouraging them in their efforts. She knows her students' names and seems to joke with them rather than reprimand them. In conversation after class, she tells you that the class assignment that day had been to explore personal space in all its movement dimensions. To do so, students had worked at their own pace according to their unique capabilities. When you tell her that you were alarmed at the hubbub, she responds that physical activity should be fun. When you tell her about the physical fitness emphasis in the school you just visited, she admits that she doesn't test her kids. However, she tells you that she encourages all of her students to aim for a higher level of fitness and health within the limitations of their own particular physiques and proclivities.

Discussion: Which school do you choose - Cartesian or Embodiment? Underlying the educational practices you can clearly see philosophy in action. During your first visit you witnessed dualism and behaviorism in action. The logical connection between the two suggests that they are linked often in educational practice. Teaching children to view their bodies as objects is dualistic. Training and testing them like little machines is behavioristic. It emphasizes the stimulus-response approach to physical education and features rewards and punishments, uniformity of tasks, conformity of behavior, measurability of results and a general disregard for the wishes and uniqueness of the children. Did you notice the following cues that this teacher had a dualistic mind-set as you watched her in front of the class? For example, she taught students

- To separate themselves into segments,

- That physical activity is mindless,

- That they must use their bodies to reach some external goal [which they may or may not find personally desirable] and,

- That their bodies may bring them rewards and success but may also be the source of humiliation and derision?

On the other hand the Embodiment School encourages students to discover their own uniqueness, to revel in the movement process and to explore their physical potential. In practice this means that teachers tend to adopt a humanistic approach to physical education. In the case that you saw, the teacher was busily encouraging every child to complete an assigned movement task to the best of their abilities. In the behavioristic class this meant completing a mindless task the teachers way and repressing individual interpretation. In the humanistic setting there was no one right way to move, each child was encouraged to add to a personal movement vocabulary to become more physically literate. The Cartesian classroom was a carefully controlled environment in which clear and specific learning outcomes were predicted and particular behavioral norms were tolerated. In the humanistic gymnasium the unexpected is expected. The creative impulse is encouraged unless it infringes upon the movement exploration of other students. In contrast to the orderly atmosphere at the first school where a strong emphasis was placed on obedience and the class was expected to work quietly and seriously, laughter was commonplace in the setting where students were encouraged to seek joy in their movement experiences. Rules existed, such as, "thou shalt stay on task" and "thou shalt not mess with other students," but within those parameters the class had great leeway to experiment, to follow their own course of action and to mingle with their peers.

The challenge you face as you contemplate embarking upon a teaching career is to clearly define your own philosophy and to consider how you might translate it into practice in the school setting.

Structuring teaching around philosophy

Discuss the following questions that are designed to help you to decide on a particular teaching environment:

1. What is your primary goal in teaching physical education? Is it to develop,

   - fitness,

   - health,

   - athletic skills,

   - the joy of movement,

   - lifetime interests,

   - physical literacy,

   - creativity,

   - self-understanding,

   - movement exploration.

   - Other

   Rank these teaching goals in order of preference

2. What would a class [or a curriculum if you prefer] look like that is developed around your number one goal?

3. How could you structure this class to emphasize the integration of mind and body?

4. How could you teach the class so that it would be dualistic?

5. What are the strengths and weaknesses of both behaviorism and humanism as philosophies of teaching physical education?

6. In which teaching environment would you feel more comfortable? Why?

Coaching with degrees of dualism

Which coaching philosophy appeals most?

After a stellar high school basketball career, you are now a senior, in the process of deciding which college to attend. You have narrowed your choice down to the two colleges that have offered you scholarships. They seem to be identical in every respect, except for the coach. You decide that your best strategy is to make a recruiting visit to check out which coach you would prefer to play for. At the College of Bill and Martha you meet Coach Carter. You are greeted warmly and invited to attend the team's practice that afternoon. To pass the time until practice is due to start, you decide to visit the athletic training facility [you had heard that there was an excellent chance that you would spend some time in the training room during your varsity career]. The athletic trainers are polite, but don't have much time to entertain any visitors that day, so you just watch what is going on for a while. A basketball player comes in with an injury. The trainer asks how the knee is and inquires how the rehabilitation program is going. "Too slow for coach," the point guard replies, "I'm needed for tonight's game." After a thorough evaluation of the injury, the trainer administers ultrasound treatment to the affected joint and leaves with the recommendation of a shot of a painkiller before the game to help play through the pain. You head up to the gym to watch the practice. Coach Carter is in the basketball office intently watching a tape of the opponent's most recent game, looking for weaknesses in the playing personnel and strategy that can be exploited in the big game tonight. Then the injured point guard arrives to give the good news, "I'm ready to play, but I don't know if the painkiller will slow me down, coach." Coach decides to make the injured player work on the jump shot, which is bound to be rusty after the long layoff.

Next, coach makes the following announcements: "The biomechanist on our staff has analyzed the latest research on the forces at work in the jump shot, the angle of trajectories and the optimal momentum. From now on we will all do it the right way - no questions asked. Furthermore, based on the physiological profiles I have just received that contain information about your respiratory endurance and body-fat levels, I have decided to institute some dietary changes and increase the number of wind sprints at each practice. Finally, I have decided to ask the sport psychologist to try something new in the hypnosis session right before the game to deaden the mind's perception of the body's pain through certain visualization techniques performed in a state of deep hypnosis. Mind over matter; that's the secret to our success tonight."

Impressed by the scientific, hi-tech approach of Coach Carter, you now depart for the College of Mary and William to size up Coach Sarter. Once again, you have time to slip down to the training room before practice. Much to your surprise, another basketball player with the same knee condition that you had witnessed on your other visit is reporting for treatment. This time though, the trainer seems less concerned with the state of the injury than with the wellbeing of the injured person. When the point guard inquires about the wisdom of returning to action for a big game that night, the trainer counsels caution: "it's up to you, but you have a lifetime to live on those legs." Upstairs, Coach Sarter is meeting with a distressed athlete who is concerned about recent poor performances. "Just relax and be yourself. Don't worry, don't force it, try to enjoy yourself," says Coach Sarter. Practice consists of the players working at their own rate on the aspects of their game that they want to work on. They seem to be absorbed in the process of play: creating new moves and practicing old techniques. Coach tells the team of some new techniques researched by sport scientists. "If they help your game, by all means use them, but remember we are all different, so don't be surprised if some of these things work better for someone else than for you. If I can be of assistance, let me know - I am here to help you to become as good as you want to be," says coach. Finally coach asks the sports psychologist to help each athlete to get in touch with their inner selves, to find peace within themselves and harmony with each other through a variety of hypnosis and visualization techniques.

At home you mull over the alternatives: will it be Carter or Sarter? To help you in your decision-making process, you make a list of key differences between the two coaches, which reads as follows:

Carter	Sarter
Knee as object [in training room also]	Knee as part of subject: concern with impact on self
Me as object: as a recruit	Me as person: emphasis on self and others
Pain of injury as a barrier to overcome	Pain as an inner signal: an opportunity to look ahead
Dependence on science and technology	Awareness of latest advances, athletes' option to use
My way or the highway: uniformity	One size does not fit all: emphasis on athlete choice
Psycho-doping: mind control as strategy	Psychology as an aid to self-awareness
Conformity as a basis of team success	Creativity and free choice for individual success
Working at the game to win	Playing at the game for self-discovery and fun

Even though you postponed the decision for as long as possible, the signing deadline eventually forced your hand. So, which coach did you decide to play for? What were the factors that swayed your decision? Would you model yourself after either of these coaches? What changes would you make before becoming either of these role models?

Discussion: To answer the basic question of how you intend to act as a coach, consider your philosophy and the philosophy underlying sport carefully. Philosophy precedes and dictates your behavior. Coach Carter's actions expressed his Cartesian leanings. When he looked at his athletes, he saw cogs in a machine. When he turned to the latest scientific research and when he adopted the most recent technological aids to performance, he was seeking greater efficiency. When he displayed impatience with injury, lack of fitness and excessive fatness, he was annoyed that the athletes were not keeping their bodies finely tuned. From this perspective, the body is something to be subjugated. Mind over matter suggests both a separation and a hierarchy. In the interests of winning the game, pain must be borne stoically. When it becomes too much to bear, coach asked the athletes to play chemical and psychological games of hide and seek with themselves by masking the pain through the use of painkillers and hypnosis. On the other hand, Coach Sarter, had a philosophy of embodiment not unlike that of Jean-Paul Sartre who believed that the body is wholly "psychic." When faced with injury, this coach and his athletic trainers recognized how the physiological breakdown is interrelated with the athlete's being. They saw that the injury was almost certainly personally devastating for college students who have so much self-esteem wrapped up in their identity as athletes. They urged caution because they were concerned that highly motivated athletes might make rash decisions to play through pain causing chronic debilitation in the future. They encouraged athletes to use medical and psychological technology to get in touch with their selves and to seek inner harmony by healing the rift that in this society, and particularly in the culture of high-performance sport, exists between mind and body. In the final analysis, the factor that may have swayed you to sign with Coach Carter is that his approach is more consistent with the prevailing philosophy of sport.

As nice as Coach Sarter seemed, his concern for your wholeness, his emphasis on athlete choice and creative fun may have seemed misplaced to you in the context of college athletics. In short, you might be concerned that such a flaky attitude is not likely to win many games. You may even be willing to overlook the ruthless attitude of Coach Carter because his focus on fitness, discipline and using every edge he can find to win games is a proven recipe for success. Dualism is implicit in such practices that bring success in sport as rigorous [mindless] practice and subjugation of your own individuality for the greater good of the team. The locker room slogan, "there is no "I" in team," reflects a level of self-alienation which might be surprising to the Sarter's of the sports world who would counter that there are "U's" and "I's" in team "unity". In no other setting, they would argue, can an individual be so totally immersed in an activity that divisions of body/mind become meaningless. In the highest level of athletic competition, you hold nothing in reserve. You are not aware of the flexing muscles, stretching ligaments and firing neurons that are enabling your movement. You are only peripherally aware of the thought processes you engage in as you notice the actions of your teammates and opponents and as you size up your strategic options. You are, at least momentarily, at one with yourself, operating in a state of unity as a lived-body. Therein lies the basic paradox in coaching today, Sarter would conclude, that this state of integration is desirable, yet so many coaching practices serve to disintegrate the moving being. As you contemplate what kind of a coach you want to be, you may find that you are faced with a fine balancing act between being co-opted by the system and living by your own philosophy. You may be content with the status quo and happy to follow in the footsteps of Coach Carter or you may decide to swim against the tide, like Coach Sarter. If so, you need determination, a thick skin and strong convictions.

Structuring coaching around philosophy

To help you in the process of thinking through your coaching philosophy to identify your convictions, consider the following discussion questions:

- In your own playing experience, have you encountered several coaches with distinct philosophies? If so, recall which coach made you feel best about yourself, who helped you to enjoy it most, who taught you most about the game and who made you the most effective player. What were the coaching qualities in each case that were successful in achieving these goals?

- Do you view yourself dualistically as you play? For example, do you analyze your technique as you play -, i.e., an inner self [mind] stepping back to evaluate the outer self [body]?

- Is it desirable to play as an embodied self?

- How would you coach differently to encourage an athlete to think and play dualistically or as an integrated whole?

- Do you side with Carter or Sarter in the debate over coaching strategy? Why?

Healing with degrees of dualism

Select the approach to healing that appeals most.

Much to your chagrin, you feel terrible. Your sore back stops you from performing well at work and at play. This state of dis-ease has persisted for months. It's time to do something about it so you visit a physical therapist. When you arrive for your appointment, Doctor Coma asks you what symptoms you are experiencing. He conducts a battery of tests before prescribing various chemicals in pill and liquid form for you to ingest for the next few months. As you leave, a parting suggestion is made that unless these medicines clear up your condition, you should undergo exploratory surgery in the next few months. You decide to visit Dr. Soma for a second opinion. In this initial examination, less time is spent on symptoms of disease than on your feelings and lifestyle. Your sense of alienation from your own body, your sense of inadequacy at work and your frustration at being unable to play seem to be of genuine concern to the therapist. After an extensive consultation, Dr. Soma suggests a course of action that includes light exercise, stretching and meditation designed to help you to heal yourself. If the problem persists, Dr. Soma counsels, a session of acupuncture may be beneficial.

Discussion: Although Doctor Soma may seem to be an anomaly in the modern western scientific medical community, the somatic approach that he represents has been prominent through time and cultural space. Historically, medicine has affirmed the intimate relationship of the mind-body and the importance of its wholeness in maintaining and restoring health. In other societies, holistic traditions of healing still dominate the medical scene, ranging from qigong, a form of self-healing exercises widely practiced in China, to shamanism among native peoples in Africa, Australia, and elsewhere. Yet in modern America, medicine has developed an exclusive focus on the physical body to which it brings a fragmentary approach. Doctor Coma would point out that this country has the most advanced medical capability in the world today.

Breakthroughs in research have allowed us to bring most of the infectious diseases that were killers in previous generations into submission. Our surgical technology and expertise is unparalleled. Doctor Soma would respectfully retort that we might have won the war with bacteria but that we are losing the battle with lifestyle. [Some hard-liners would not even concede that we have been victorious in germ warfare, pointing out that we may have won the first battle but that the war is still raging as the depleted ranks of the microbes are even now being reinforced by treatment-resistant mutations].

Most people in America today die of lifestyle-related diseases, ranging from heart conditions, cancer, and AIDS to automobile accidents and homicides. Even when an individual has a genetic predisposition to one of these potentially lethal conditions, changes in the lifestyle can often help to delay, and perhaps even prevent, the onset of the disease. Even so, the old school of treatment, represented here by Doctor Coma, treats the body not the being, looks for symptoms not causes and advocates chemical intervention and surgery not natural methods of healing, such as herbal therapy, meditation and exercise. The alternative is for physicians to become healers by exchanging the role of all-knowing purveyors of medical knowledge, diviners of symptoms and dispensers of pharmaceutical remedies for that of the counselor. Instead of telling patients what to do and to take in order to get better, the role of the physician would change to that of friend and facilitator in the changing paradigm of healing. Such a change would hasten the societal shift from disease treatment to disease prevention and health promotion that is currently evident in the growth of wellness programs in such institutions as hospitals, businesses and colleges.

Underlying this change in the paradigm of health and healing is the cultural evolution of mind-body philosophy. The Cartesian distinctions between consciousness and matter are becoming blurred. It is not the body that gets sick and needs help, it is the whole human organism. Conventional remedies will continue to cure bacterially based infections and to surgically replace degenerating organs, but increasingly disease is being recognized as a symptom of a psychosomatic condition. The term psychosomatic can be interpreted as the mind working on the body to cause or cure some debilitating condition, which implies a separation even as they work in a tandem, or it can mean a total embodiment: the concept of a unified source of health, of energy, of being. As an alternative to the impersonal, alienating nature of endless high-tech scans and tests of modern medicine, many seek the solace of psychosomatic remedies in the offices of alternative therapists and faith healers - to the tune of $30 billion a year, by some estimates.

Your mind-body philosophy is going to radically affect your attitudes to the profession, whether you select a career in the health and healing fields or you only come into contact with the medical community as a patient.

Is holistic healing for you?

The following discussion topics are designed to help you to develop your own position:

- To what extent do you consider your body to be the source of your disease?

- Do you know of any cases where the mind played a prominent role in recovery from a debilitating condition?

- Have you experienced any psychosomatic ailments?

- Can you name any effective psychosomatic treatments?

- Should the physician determine symptoms and treatment for the patient?

- To what extent should self-help be a part of the cure?

- Do such concepts as shared consciousness and vital energy have meaning?

- If so, can they play a role in the healing process?

Exercise 2-12: Research

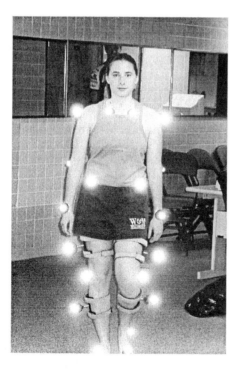

Choices in dualism

After graduating from college with sterling credentials, you decide to satisfy your longing to extend the boundaries of knowledge by seeking employment in a research field. The first interview you have is with a large pharmaceutical company that is engaged in a search for a cure for AIDS. The particular project they want you to join entails injecting chimpanzees with the disease and studying the effectiveness of various experimental sera. They may be the closest relative to mankind, but they are only animals, the interviewer reassures you.

Next, you consider working for a biotechnology company which is studying the effects of the human growth hormone on children. The experimental protocol is to inject the hormone into live human tissue in various dosages to study effectiveness and side effects.

Next you are off to a large agricultural combine where you will be asked to research hormonal and chemical additives that will bring meat on the hoof to fruition in a shorter time and in a more tender state.

Finally, you have an interview with a sports performance enhancement company. At last, you think with a sigh of relief, a chance to work with healthy people. The interviewer explains that you will be extracting blood to study lactate levels during exercise and fibers to evaluate the muscle's response to stress. Assuming similar working conditions, salary and benefits, which job would you take? Why?

Visions of holism

From these interview fragments, what can you deduce about the following questions concerning scientific research on the body?

- Is the body treated as an object to be probed, dissected and analyzed?

- Do you think that the objectification of the body somehow justifies experimental treatment that would be considered demeaning to a person?

- Do you think that the rights of animals are secondary to the health and wellbeing of mankind in that if they can save us from getting sick and provide us with sustenance, any research measures are justifiable?

Discussion: The style of science is reductionism. Its basic methodology is to focus on one aspect of the body, isolating it from all else, controlling everything impinging on it and measuring everything that happens. Science has enabled us to look at the body and gain insights, but ones that are fragmented into bits and pieces. The assumption of reductionist research is that if the body can be reduced to its most basic parts and if these parts can be understood, then a comprehensive explanation of human performance will eventually be obtained by simply fitting the components back together like pieces in a giant jigsaw puzzle.

What are the limitations of this method of studying the body in order to understand movement? For one, we cannot know anything with certainty, only with statistical significance. The very act of observing the body changes it. To study it we must control it. Therefore, we can never really know the body as it really is. But, the shortcoming that is most important is that the study of the nature of the body cannot account for human nature. A human moving is not synonymous with a body in motion. Scientific research can enhance human performance, but it has its shortcomings. Consider the following examples: digitized computer analysis to improve the quarterback's throwing technique, gait analysis on a force platform to help the elderly to move more freely or altitude stress-testing to determine how the human body will respond to the rigors of mountain climbing. Each is a valuable contribution to our knowledge of how the body functions. However, they are all meaningless in the absence of the vitality and vigor of being in the body. Despite the statistical predictions of how our bodies should respond to different stimuli under various conditions, we are each unique. Feelings, moods and qualities of character differentiate predictable behavior from the reality of our reaction.

The self-understanding that comes from philosophic reflection should be the starting place and the destination of experimentation. If you enter the world of scientific research, awareness of the dualism, fragmentation, uses and abuses of the process will prepare you for the professional challenges ahead. Research findings can be useful to humanity within the limitations already discussed, but they have a value in the marketplace and, sometimes, in the battlefield, that renders them vulnerable to the problems of commodification. They can be used for profit, for personal gain, to help (but sometimes to hurt) others. In other words, it is incumbent upon you as a philosophically mature researcher to ask such questions as, knowledge for what purposes, for what uses and at what cost? With such questions in mind, you can choose wisely at your job interviews and embark upon a career dedicated to expanding knowledge of the nature of things and of your self.

Research and the body-object

Is the body objectified in a research setting? Read the following description of being in an anatomy lab and respond to the questions.

" As a college student in your first human anatomy class, you make an incision with your scalpel, pull the skin back from the abdomen and cautiously slip your hands inside the cadaver. You are at the same time excited at the prospect of learning about the human body through exploring it yourself and slightly nauseated by the whole experience. Perhaps your distaste is partly due to the sights (of withered flesh and exposed innards) and the smells (of formaldehyde and body fluids). But even more upsetting than these physical sensations is your stark realization that this ugly hunk of human remnants lying before you used to be a person. Despite the reassurances of the professor that this is just a cadaver, a body that has been donated to science, you cannot rid yourself of the knowledge that this thing was someone, who much like you had hopes and dreams. You find yourself wondering what this class is teaching you about the human body as an object as you rummage around in previously private places."

- Does this description resonate with your own experience?

- How are anatomy labs dualistic?

- Can you give examples of practices in education, health care and sport that are similarly dualistic?

- Is there an alternative approach that would humanize those professions based on a more holistic philosophy?

- Is it desirable for students of human movement to take a more holistic approach?

- What would kinesiology look like if it were to be restructured to be more holistic?

- How would such a shift change the perception of kinesiology in higher education?

- Would such a shift benefit society?

Review

A paramount goal of applied philosophy is to enhance your self-understanding. By now, you should be aware of different ways of understanding and the role that your movement activities can play in expanding your awareness of your self. A major component in this process is mind/body dualism. Cartesian dualism colors the way you see yourself, the way you move, the way you approach relationships, even the way you earn a living. In this chapter we explored this mind/body relationship along a continuum from the extremes of dualistic thinking to the realms of embodied consciousness. After this review, we can see the power of philosophy. A change in our self-perception can affect our thinking, our moving, our very being.

Chapter 3

UNDERSTANDING OTHERS

Preview

Developing your philosophy entails considering all alternatives carefully as you craft your own world-view. Reaching philosophic maturity is not just part of the process of growing older, it is a struggle which you must knowingly enter and win. The closed mind and the narrow mind are twin combatants that you may have to fight. The attitude of the closed mind is that you refuse to think about alternative visions of reality because you have already made up your mind. The narrow mind resists ideas that might challenge the status quo and it rejects ideas that emanate from other ethnic groups, subcultures and cultures than those to which you have been exposed as you matured. They are both the offspring of security and complacency. It is too easy to proclaim that we can find the answers to our existence in the snug little world in which we have been reared. The challenge of this chapter is to step beyond the comfortable confines of your cultural perspective and to explore uncharted philosophical terrain. In this process of discovery, you might find that your preconceived notions are threatened. If so, you will have the opportunity to test your own philosophic maturity. If you are ready to grow, you will adopt ideas that make sense to you and adapt your philosophy to synthesize those ideas that are salient, even though they were once alien to your way of thinking.

The particular world that we are going to enter in this chapter is the mysterious and mystic Orient. It is a world that we rarely mention in philosophic texts published in the western world because westerners can neither fully understand nor clearly explain the ideas and practices we encounter in the East. Paradoxically, traditional eastern ways are finding their way into western culture despite this lack of scholarly attention. Martial arts (such as judo and karate) and meditative pastimes (such as yoga and tai chi) are booming. Eastern medical methods, (such as herbal treatment and acupuncture) are increasingly popular. In this chapter, we will encounter the philosophy that permeates and explains these practices. As we pass through this philosophic universe of brands of Buddhism, most notably Taoism and Zen, we will explore the inexplicable, for example the "artless art" and the pursuit of purposelessness, the mastery of chi and the mystery of the meridians. You may be tempted to throw up your arms in despair at the alien nature of these concepts. Yet, features of our everyday existence are ineffable too. In another chapter we will struggle to understand and define beauty in movement. Because our efforts lead to partial success at best, we will not therefore declare that beauty either does not exist or is not important. Similarly, the phenomena we are about to encounter are very real to millions of people. We could dismiss them out of hand because we can neither understand nor explain them, or we could resist the temptation to be narrow or closed-minded by being open to the consideration of these new ideas.

Encountering Eastern Philosophy

Eastern philosophy is an all-encompassing term. How far east are we talking? Certainly well beyond the eastern seaboard of the United States and far beyond eastern Europe. Specifically we are discussing philosophies that have dominated thinking in Asia for centuries. Just as in the western world a range of philosophies and religious beliefs coexist, the eastern world is heavily influenced by the diverse belief-systems of Moslem, Hinduism and Buddhism. Buddhism, and its' derivatives Confucianism, Taoism and Jainism are the focus of this discussion. Buddhism began in 534 B.C. when Siddhartha Gautama, the historic Buddha, at the age of 29 renounced his wife and his family possessions to discover the cause of human suffering and its cure through self-mortification, self-discipline and meditation. Since that time, Buddhism has spread through China, Japan, Korea, southeastern Asia, Sri Lanka, Burma and Tibet. In a nutshell, the historic Buddha realized that everything is subject to change and that suffering and discontent are the result of attachment to circumstances and things that, by their nature, are impermanent. By ridding oneself of these attachments, including attachments to the false notion of self, one can be free of suffering. These teachings of Buddha have been passed down through the generations and through different eastern cultures from teacher to student.

The belief-system is not restricted to the eastern world. Its ideas have been attractive to many in the western world. Such European existentialists as Liebnitz, Hegel, Kierkegaard and Jaspers expressed interest in Buddhist philosophy because it resonates with their belief that existence precedes essence. Others have found aspects of Buddhism seductive because it poses an alternative to the fast paced, stressful, materialistic cultures of the west. Meditation, a mainstay of the contemplative life, relieves stress and allows many the opportunity to find their own space and dictate their own pace in an otherwise frenetic lifestyle. Today, Buddhism, in its many forms, is practiced in all western countries, and the number of adherents to its philosophy is growing steadily.

Why are eastern philosophies and practices finding a foothold in the western world? One answer to this question is that the children of the Information Age are realizing that while information may bring knowledge, it does not guarantee wisdom, nor does it lead to self-understanding. Bombarded with information from all sources, westerners gather knowledge at an astonishing rate and struggle to assimilate it into their belief-system and lifestyle. From the eastern perspective, knowledge must be accompanied by an experience or it is superficial - someone else's knowledge. Through experience comes wisdom providing we see intuitively, we abandon subject/object dichotomies and we grasp the wholeness or oneness of reality. Only then can we grasp the unity that leads to wisdom and self-understanding. In Buddhist terms this search for Enlightenment is accomplished by adhering to the four noble truths and following the 8-fold path. The four noble truths may be summarized as:

1. The essence of existence is suffering

2. The origin of suffering is desire, craving, grasping

3. Suffering will cease if we can eliminate this desire

4. Desire may be eliminated if we follow the 8-fold path

The 8-fold path entails living the life of the golden mean, by having:

1. Right views

2. Right aspirations

3. Right speech

4. Right conduct

5. Right means of livelihood

6. Right effort

7. Right mindfulness

8. Right contemplation and meditation.

Buddhists believe that adopting this lifestyle will lead to the cessation of craving, to truth and to ultimate insight. They believe that through self and mental discipline, things may be discovered as they really are, not as they appear to be. Through meditation comes enlightenment. As one popular saying suggests, "Look within, thou art the Buddha". (Buddha means "enlightened or awakened one"). Zen Buddhism, in particular, has found a following in the west because it emphasizes a search for the Buddha nature in oneself - a search for ultimate knowledge beyond the apparent world of change. It offers stability in an otherwise ephemeral transitory existence, where the only constant is change. To paraphrase this belief consider the following illustration from Taoism (Tao is the Path or the way). To follow the path is to practice going against the stream, not by struggling against it and thrashing, but by standing still and letting the stream do the work. The Tao is a way of harmony, interaction and cooperation. The sage knows that, relative to the river, he still moves against the current. The sage, or master, does not encourage suffering by struggling against the forces of nature but seeks reconciliation between matter and spirit, the finite world and absolute reality and the one and the many. The Zen search for enlightenment is through the everyday mind: "sleeping when tired, eating when hungry". It is very different to the western mind-set, which applauds "go-getters" who go out and make things happen. In the place of ambition (make your mark!) is acceptance (let it be!). What western philosophy applauds (reflecting, deliberating and conceptualizing), eastern philosophy avoids because the original unconsciousness would be lost when a thought interferes. The eastern perspective emphasizes the unity of all things, the yin and the yang as one all-encompassing force.

This unity, or balance, is illustrated by the symbol of an interlocking, overlapping flow of movement within a circle. The similar, and at the same time contrasting, energies are moving together in a symbiotic relationship. Within the black area there is a white dot and within the white area, there is a black dot. This circle illustrates the cyclical nature of existence and shows that within a unity there is duality and polarity and contrast. It suggests that the way to find real balance without losing the centering feeling of the circle is to think of the contrasting energies moving together and in union as a kind of consummation between two forces, male and female, mind and body, good and bad. The Yin is inert and passive, while the Yang is free-moving and active. Trying to balance these opposite tendencies, which we all possess, is the goal of life. The yin-yang symbol illustrates not only the duality of our existence, but also the harmony of the interlocking elements, the importance of achieving and maintaining a balance.

Life force, vital energy or chi is crucial to the existence of all that lives. Chi is mysterious. You can go your whole life dependent on it without even being aware of its existence. It is ubiquitous. It animates, integrates and pervades everything that exists. It suffuses the very waters of life. It is probably chi that takes your single sock from the washing machine. Chi provides the intrinsic force necessary in your blood to keep you alive. It is the force of nature that makes the grass grow, the planet turn and the sunburn. Chi flows through your body via a complex network of channels called meridians, which bear no resemblance to the geography of the human body as we know it in the west. These meridians are connected throughout the body by the fingers, feet, chest, face and shoulders. The meridians travelling in the dorsal and lateral regions are considered yang, and those running in the ventral region and on the inner side of the limbs are considered yin. When its flow is unobstructed you enjoy good total health (physical, emotional, psychological, spiritual, etc.) When its flow is impeded you get sick. When it stops, you die. Achieving balance between yin and yang, and maximizing the flow of chi is the goal of movement and medicine.

Review and Preview

So far, we have learned that a significant number of the inhabitants of this globe believe and act in ways very foreign to western culture. In particular, their philosophical beliefs about the meaning of life and the purpose of our existence seem to be contrary to societal norms that most westerners have grown up with. Because all actions stem from our philosophy, practices that we may tend to take for granted are profoundly different in cultures based on widely divergent belief systems.

In the next section we will consider the implications and applications of eastern philosophy for western society. In particular, we will focus upon health and healing and sport and moving. In both cases, we will encounter ideas and practices that will challenge our traditional ways. This process is designed to help you to become more philosophically mature. This process entails reacting to the alien ways, distancing your self from the ideas you are encountering to facilitate objectivity and identifying features that seem unusual and even threatening to your beliefs. More importantly, it should culminate in you analyzing the validity of eastern philosophy and practice and, where applicable, synthesizing its salient features into your own understanding

Implications of Eastern Philosophy for Western Society

There is a natural tendency when we encounter other cultures to be ethnocentric: to judge things foreign to us from our own ingrained cultural perspective. As we have seen earlier in this text, the philosophic process is one of analysis and synthesis. If you have not passed beyond the reacting stage, you will be quick to judge and condemn these alien concepts. If, however, you are maturing (philosophically speaking) you will analyze these alien notions and synthesize those that you can accept and understand into your belief-system. Learning to question yourself as a product of your own culture is a big step toward self-understanding.

Overcoming Ethnocentrism

Only by stepping outside of our own worldview can we truly appreciate the perspectives of other cultures. This process involves the critical analysis of our own ways of "doing business". The following exercises are designed to help us to overcome ethnocentricism, to better appreciate the philosophy of others by putting our own belief-systems under the philosophical microscope. After the process of analysis is complete, a synthesis of different philosophic perspectives is a more reasonable expectation.

Exercise 3-1: Imbalance in western thought

Try taking a critical look at the way we live from an eastern perspective by answering the following question in light of the discussion that follows:

Do we over-emphasize the yang and neglect the yin in western society?

Signs of this imbalance would be that we revere masculine values over feminine, that we are too rational, scientific, aggressive and competitive - a culture that neglects the intuitive, religious, compassionate and cooperative.

Discussion: If you respond positively to this question, you probably see that we live in a patriarchal society. You might ascribe to the theories of hegemony, which suggest that social forces are at play in our culture to maintain the dominant white male power structure. You might think that we seem to be more eager to make war than to make peace, both personally and politically. You might suspect that there are other ways to truth than through the processes of intellectualization and science.

agree

· Raising children
frowned upon
· Compassion lost for goals

π - other class discussion
→ other cultures → Colombia
"always late"

Exercise 3-2: Fragmentation in western thought

The eastern perspective emphasizes the balanced unity of all things, the yin and yang as one all-encompassing force. Do you think that western society is not only unbalanced, but also severely fragmented?

Discussion: To say yes here, you probably believe that because we are heavily influenced by Cartesian dualism we tend to identify success with our minds (which is a distinct, detached ego existing within the body). You may view the body as a tool (perhaps leading to abuses to make the body perform better) or as an obstacle (possibly leading to health problems such as anorexia nervosa and bulimia). You might see that this sense of fragmentation extends beyond our perceptions of self to color the way we view others as a fragmented grouping of events and objects. This view causes the separation of races, religions, nations and political groups in society and results in alienation among mankind. This can lead to an unfair distribution of resources, political and economic disorder and violence. You might extend this alienation to the westerners isolation from nature. The Taoist tradition is deeply rooted in a respect for Nature and universal union with the natural order. A strong emphasis within western capitalist cultures tends to be to hold dominion over Nature, to conquer and control, to cultivate, to use and, sometimes, to exploit the environment for profit and for pleasure. If so, you might give credence to a philosophy of fragmentation as the cause of an abuse of natural resources and pollution resulting in an unhealthy environment.

The eastern view that perceives all things as connected, interrelated and part of the same unified whole offers a direct contrast to this fragmented western perspective. Eastern mysticism sees a universal wholeness, in that all things are different aspects or manifestations of the same reality. In this world view, it is merely illusion to see oneself as an isolated ego with the power to forge your own way through life, or to perceive the things and events of this world as separate and disconnected. The underlying problem of this perspective, described in the Buddhist tradition as avidya (which means disturbed mind), is that the western mentality is to categorize and measure. This tendency leads to limitations in our thinking. If it doesn't fit into the categories of understanding that we have established, then it is either marginalized or dismissed altogether as valid knowledge. This is a critical difference between the eastern and western perspectives because it influences the mode of thought of the two cultures. The eastern and western traditions have inverted ways of knowing. The west has emphasized rational thought over intuition and scientific knowledge over a form of spiritual enlightenment. The eastern tradition has been just the opposite.

For western thought, abstraction is an important part of rational knowledge because we cannot consider all the features of the numerous structures and phenomena of our physical reality, but must instead focus on a select few features. Thus, rational knowledge is an understanding of abstract symbols and concepts and is organized into a linear, sequential system characteristic of western thought and speech. Furthermore, rational thought is limited to the features of these abstractions and the degree of their relativity to known and explicable phenomena. Because this rational abstraction of reality is easier to understand than reality itself, the western tendency has been to mistake these abstract concepts and symbols for reality itself. Eastern mysticism seeks the truth of the reality that lies beyond rational abstract concepts and symbols. Consequently, words used to convey eastern philosophy are rarely precise, but are often presented as parables, which illustrate, but don't define the concept in question. This is not because of any limitation of vocabulary, but because the reality transcends the descriptive instrumentality of words. Where the western mind tends to break knowledge up into bite-sized chunks, so that it is easily digestible, the eastern mentality is to wrestle with the big picture on it's own terms. The eastern mystic believes that the ultimate reality can never be understood by rationalization, nor can it be explained by words or demonstrated to another person:

Applications of Eastern Philosophy in Western Society

Eastern practices are visibly different from their counterparts in the west. We tend not to think about philosophy when we do things, such as sport, art and medicine. However, it would be a mistake to divorce the activity from the philosophy when we try to understand different eastern ways, because philosophy and practice are inextricably interwoven into the conduct of these activities. Some westerners have made that mistake. They have imported the practice without the meaning behind it. In some cases, martial arts, such as judo and karate have been taught as competitive sports, with the sole intent of winning, and as means of combat, with the intent of causing harm by attacking another. As we shall see, the purpose of these activities in their native setting is not to win, but to seek another goal, not to intentionally hurt another but to defend against the attack of an aggressor. In the east, more so than in western culture, philosophy and practice integrate one's physical, cultural, mental and spiritual dimensions. Hybrid forms of eastern thought permeate western culture. However, we rarely encounter them in the natural state of their native habitat. As such activities as judo and karate cross the oceans, they tend to lose their authenticity. Most of the ensuing discussion will focus on the "real McCoy", but before entering the eastern world, here is an exercise to help you to consider the prevalence of eastern thought in western culture today.

Exercise 3-3: Eastern thought in western practice

Eastern ideas are not alien to our culture. In fact they are increasingly permeating our thoughts and our activities. Consider the impact of eastern thought in each of the following categories: sport, medicine and popular culture. Here is a table designed to help you to catalog these activities:

	Medicine	Sport	Popular Culture
Name of activity			
Description How is this activity conducted? Indicate if you are describing the activity from first hand experience.			
Distinguishing Features What distinguishes the conduct of this eastern activity from the conduct of traditional western activities in this category?			

After you have listed the particular examples that come to mind, describe the qualities of these eastern activities and then differentiate them from traditionally western activities in each category. We have already mentioned martial arts and acupuncture as examples in the first two columns, but to illustrate how western thought is permeating popular culture, there follows a description of two such items, drawn from the genres of books and film.

Exercise 3-4: Eastern thought in western literature

Consider the popular tales of Winnie the Pooh, not only as entertaining stories for children, but also as an example of eastern philosophy, and answer the following questions:

1. How many features can you find in these tales that resemble and resonate with the eastern philosophic approaches discussed in this chapter?

2. To what extent do you think that this eastern flavor accounts for the popularity of these stories in western culture?

Discussion: The following discussion should help you to answer these questions. Examples of eastern thought in popular literature abound. The example that will be included here is a more recent attempt to infuse eastern ideas into a popular childrens story: *The Tao of Pooh*, by Benjamin Hoff. An example of the thought process that you might go through as you complete this exercise is provided by a College of William and Mary student, Susan, who critiques the Tao off Pooh as follows:

"In his work, Hoff takes the lovable and laid-back Winnie the Pooh, along with the other characters, such as Tigger, Piglet and Eeyore and uses them to explain the Chinese way of thinking. The story of Winnie the Pooh provides an excellent example to illustrate Eastern thought because it is written in a way that a student brought up in the Western world can understand. Nearly everyone can relate to the characters in Winnie the Pooh. We all know of an Eeyore, always sad and depressed, and a Piglet who is afraid of his own shadow. Most of us also know someone who shares the characteristics of the Owl, who is always finding the answers in a book, and of the Rabbit, who is a workaholic. But Pooh, in contrast, just goes with the flow rather than showing one particular character trait. He does not fight the Tao, he just flows. As such, he is happy and content. For example, one particular day, Pooh gets up and walks through the Hundred Acre Wood wondering what he would do that day, when he sees Rabbit rushing around as usual. When Pooh asked him why he was in such a hurry, Rabbit responded, "Don't you know what today is?"" No", said Pooh. "It's Wednesday," replied Rabbit. "Oh, it is", says Pooh, "then I shall wish everyone a happy Wednesday." Which he proceeds to do."

Susan continues her analysis by pointing out that the primary characteristics of Taoism that are demonstrated in the charming tales of Winnie the Pooh can be translated into the larger arena of life:

"This is how Taoists live. They find the beauty of life in Nature and try to flow and conduct themselves in the way that Nature does. When you discard arrogance and complexity, sooner or later you will discover that simple, childlike and mysterious secret known to those of the Uncarved Block: Life is Fun. The Uncarved Block is Taoism's symbol of the perfection of the natural state of things. Tao roughly translates as "way", referring to that which happens of itself along the way or Great Thoroughfare of Life. This applies as much to the landing of a ladybug upon your summer shirt as it does to the formation of the Universe. Underlying, and running in the cracks and spaces between reality, the Tao is the primary generative force of existence, and for that matter, non-existence."

Exercise 3-5: Eastern philosophy in western movies

Eastern thought permeates the popular culture of western countries. Answer the following questions to indicate the level of saturation in this particular example and in the movie industry generally:

1. Consider the Star wars series in particular. How is the following phrase associated with the movie an example of eastern thought: May the Force be with you!

2. Identify other features of this movie that make you think of eastern ideas. The following discussion is included to help you with this identification process.

3. List other movies that contain eastern perspectives. Go beyond such obvious choices as the Karate Kid series to assess eastern thought presented in western packages.

Discussion: A striking parallel can be observed between Zen Buddhist philosophy and the Force, as depicted in Star Wars. In the following analysis, another student, Geoff, probes this relationship:

" A Jedi Master is the movie equivalent of a Zen master. Jedi masters have supreme control over the power of the Force. Ben Kenobie, a Jedi knight, says of the force:

"The Force is what gives a Jedi his power. It's an energy field created by all living things. It surrounds us and penetrates us. It binds the galaxy together."

Immediately, a parallel structure begins to appear between Zen Buddhism and the Force. A master is the only one who can both teach and draw from a greater cosmic power. In the movie, Luke Skywalker aspires to be a Jedi Knight, a process which closely resembles the training of the Japanese Samurai warriors according to the exacting code of Bushido, which emphasized duty, honor and service in the name of good. The movies also depict Luke's struggle to attain mastery over the Force. This is a tedious process that requires a great deal of training and the guidance of a Jedi Master. Initially Yoda, the Jedi master, refuses to teach Luke the ways of the Force because, 'the boy has no patience". Patience is an integral component of mastering the Force, just as it is integral to mastering Zen Buddhism. Luke struggles with his lack of patience just as he struggles with the path to enlightenment in the ways of the Force. He continually asks Yoda questions, but Yoda refuses to give straight answers because Luke must experience the spiritual philosophy for himself. One such exchange goes like this:

> LUKE: But tell me why I can't...
>
> YODA: (interrupting) No, no, there is no why. Nothing more will I teach you today. Clear your mind of questions. You must be calm, at peace. Passive.'

Luke is told that he will 'feel the Force flowing through him' once he has tapped into this spiritual power of the Universe. During a climactic scene when Luke is nearing the completion of his training, he complains that he is unable to progress further in his understanding of the Force. He feels that what he understands is different from what Yoda, his Master, is trying to teach him. Yoda says,

> 'No! No different! Only different in your mind. You must unlearn what you have learned.for my ally is the Force. And a powerful ally it is. Life creates it, makes it grow. Its energy surrounds us and binds

us. Luminous beings are we (Yoda pinches Luke's shoulder) not this crude matter (he makes a sweeping gesture) You must feel the Force around you. Here, between you, me, the tree, the rock, everywhere.'

This advice encapsulates the Zen Buddhist philosophy that enlightenment is achieved through the experience of becoming one with the energy that connects the cosmos, that resides in everything. However, the best illustration is when Yoda uses his mastery of the Force to move an entire space ship. Luke says in amazement that he does not believe what Yoda was able to do. Yoda's simple reply is 'that is why you fail'. Examined in a larger context, this scene depicts Luke's inability to rid himself of his preconceived notions of what is possible and what is not. To Luke, Yoda seems to be describing abstract ideas. Luke is even skeptical of the feats that Yoda is able to perform."

Exercise 3-6: Problems of perception

Influence of parents → betrayal to them

Try as we might, we can never completely overcome ethnocentricism. On one hand, we can never fully shed our cultural skins. Our world-view is always going to be influenced by our upbringing, by our significant others and by our society. Similarly, we can never fully grasp a thought process that is alien to us. Answer the following questions designed to help you to assess what you cannot comprehend:

1. List the qualities of eastern thinking that you find difficulty to fully understand or appreciate.

2. How do the literature and movie examples that you have identified as being eastern help you to bridge this gulf of understanding?

Discussion: Once again, it may help you to read how a student started to tackle these thorny issues: Geoff reflected upon the gulf that separates the western mind in general (and his own in particular) from the eastern experience:

Pooh: simplify

" Luke's attitude is a wonderful portrayal of the western skepticism that influences me. Ironically, this inability to accept, to free the body to experience, to unlearn the learned, is what prevents Luke, and westerners like me from grasping the Force, or Zen Buddhism. For me, Star Wars is a tangible gateway for understanding Eastern philosophy. These movies place Eastern concepts into a western context. They become tangible, something I can begin to see and hear. Despite the fact that these concepts are portrayed in a very 'Hollywood' fashion, there can be little doubt that they contain numerous elements of eastern philosophy. After viewing these movies again to refresh my memory, I find myself very excited by the numerous points of contact between Zen Buddhism and the concepts depicted in the movies. Luke's progress from skeptic to Jedi Knight demonstrates the process of unlearning, experience and faith that one must undergo to experience Zen Buddhism. Luke, as a skeptical western counterpart, provided the link that enabled me to look within myself and see what changes must take place for me to gain, at the very least, a greater understanding of what Zen Buddhists try to describe and encourage others to experience."

Exercise 3-7: Western philosophy and eastern practice

In contrast to previous exercises in which you have identified connections between eastern thought and western cultural practice, it is now time to pinpoint the differences:

1. Identify how western popular culture distorts eastern thought. Give examples of the fundamental differences between the ways that eastern thought is presented in the books and movies you have discussed and the essence of eastern philosophy.

2. How have eastern healing practices that are becoming popular in the west changed or ignored traditional eastern thought?

Discussion: The sports that we do, the medical treatments we seek, the books we read and the movies we see are all formative influences. We become socialized to their norms and we develop a belief-system around their ideology. Carried along the ever-widening information highway, alternative cultural perspectives are absorbed into our culture and, ultimately, into our philosophy. However, as these ideas migrate from their source to reach us, they change. The eastern philosophy that has helped to form eastern practice is often ignored when these activities reach western society. In many cases the reason for making such changes is in order to make them more palatable. They change because we interpret them according to our own understandings of reality.

We will now travel back to the source to visit these ideas in their unadulterated pristine condition as we think about movement and medicine.

The Art and Science of Movement and Medicine

When you think of movement in western society, you probably think of sport. The goal of most sports is to win. The means of winning is competing. To compete and win, athletes are taught the values of carefully thinking through and implementing a strategy. To be successful, you must be deliberate, almost scientific in your approach. Sport in the west is tactical and rational. The reward is often beyond the act itself. It may take the form of fame and fortune or conquest and kudos. Sport in the west reflects the acquisitive, comparative face of capitalism. It pits athlete against athlete, team against team to see who is stronger. It is a physical struggle of survival in which there can only be one winner.

In contrast, physical activity in the east is an art. From martial arts to the art of archery, the goal is to seek enlightenment, not to vanquish an opponent. To accomplish this goal, the art must become artless. The participant becomes purposeless and egoless through the meditative centering process. The purpose of finding one's center is to restore the balance of vital energy in the body. The purpose of these arts is not to win or to be the strongest or fastest, but rather to open oneself to a deeper level of consciousness in which the very nature of oneself can be experienced. This state, where intention and action are simultaneous and the participant finds inner enlightenment is known by such terms as satori or nirvana, (depending upon the eastern tradition). It is from the eastern tradition that we have taken such ideas as that the purpose of the contest is to take aim at and hit yourself as well as the target. Thus, the true goal is self-discovery through connectedness with nature and through childlikeness. The state to strive for in, and through, eastern activity is childlikeness. A child is natural, close to nature. We should seek to be a part of it, to learn from its ways and be wise. Nature is the ultimate model and is often used as an analogy to explain how we should behave.

Movement is a part of every day life in the east, not a pastime or an extra-curricular activity as it tends to be in western culture, but an essential fixture in the daily regimen. It has a different degree of significance than sport and athletics in western cultures because the rewards are of a more spiritual nature. Instead of rational thought, the eastern belief is that direct intuition is the only way to experience the enlightenment of knowing the ultimate reality. The main purpose of all schools of eastern mysticism is to prepare the mind for this awareness of reality. This silencing of the mind can be achieved in meditation by concentrating on one's breathing, the vision of a mandala, or the sound of a mantra. This state of mind can also be experienced through exercises that allow one to focus attention on spontaneous body movements performed without the interference of thought. This concept of acting without thinking may seem curious to a culture reared on the admonition to "look before you leap". Typically, we plan our course of action before we embark upon it, but the Zen way is to allow the course of events to unfold rather than to make things happen. The influence of Zen on the Japanese samurai led to the development of bushido (the way of the warrior). The samurai warrior, through this art of swordsmanship, is able to achieve the highest level of spiritual insight.

One of the most spiritual martial arts, which is often referred to as "moving Zen", is aikido, which translates into "the way of harmony of spirit". This Japanese martial art, which was developed by Moriei Ueshiba, focuses on using the energy of the opponent to gain control of him. Ueshiba intended that aikido would be a vehicle to reach spiritual perfection through training awareness and unity of mind. As in karate, kyudo, t'ai chi and the tea ceremony, the aikido practitioner seeks equanimity of the mind, a spontaneous action and response and the development of an ability to perceive the reality of things as they are. The aikido method of training involves the repetition of fundamental movements and establishing and preserving mindfulness in practice. The cooperative nature of aikido rejects the competitive nature of western sport that reinforces self/other dichotomies. This cooperation also establishes in the practitioner a concern for others' wellbeing and safety that should be carried throughout life. Since the goal of the aikido practitioner is to create the state of mind that allows the experience of a balanced, harmonized self, the first order of business is to balance the"in" and "yo", which are the aikido equivalents of yin and yang. Thus, if there is a hard, fast attack (yo), it must be balanced by an equal reaction of a soft, fast acceptance (in). The "in" and "yo" cannot exist without each other. Every aikido technique must incorporate both. The process of balancing can result in a violent eruption of forces trying to equalize, but when harmony is finally achieved the result is an extraordinary beauty. The beauty is in the union of mind/body, of partners and of man with nature. Through the movements of aikido, participants seek the unity and harmony that are prerequisite to understand reality and the ultimate truth.

The Way to Tao is not through knowing and doing, but rather through not knowing and non-doing. This opens the door to Tao. Taoism has a long history of involvement in exercise and movement techniques. When performed in the traditional way, tai chi chuan is a form of moving meditation. The source for movement is not an exertion of muscle strength, but the power of the chi. Through diligent practice, it is claimed that one can move with tranquility as chi circulates through the body. Tai chi stimulates the central nervous system, lowers blood pressure and relieves stress, while gently toning the muscles without strain. It also enhances digestion and blood circulation as the rhythmic movements massage the internal organs and help to improve their functionality. At one level, tai chi is a form of healthy exercise, but in reality it is much more. It is a complete way of life, a way of being, wherein a person's inner life and outer experience become unified as a single expression of existence of the Tao. The exercises in tai chi combine the mind, breath, balance and parts of the body to work simultaneously and spontaneously during each movement. Tai chi, like all eastern disciplines, is a way of approaching the whole of life and thus must be practiced every second of the day. As an answer to the condition of separation and conflict in which humanity finds itself, the Chinese developed a combination of physical and spiritual exercises to aid the practitioner in obtaining an intuitive understanding of, and oneness with, the Tao. These were based on close observation of the world around them and the principles that underlay the continuous movement of the Tao. The ancient Chinese classic, the Tao Te Ching contains the ideas and principles from which the tai chi disciplines were derived. The movements of tai chi are an imitation of the movements of the Tao. They are closely allied to the movements of nature. Imitation is a form of unity through which the tai chi practitioner aims to gain harmony with all things. Tai chi requires total absorption. In other words, it must be done totally with all one's being in a process where the distinction between mind, body and soul is lost as they flow into each other and merge in harmony. It must be a process where consciousness is dispersed from the mind throughout every cell of the body, so that the entire being becomes pure awareness. Hand, foot, breath, balance and concentration blend into each other until the individual disappears into the void that is the Tao. In the void the ego is no more. There is only spontaneous, unceasing harmonious movement. Tai chi is an unending journey toward oneself and toward Oneness with all things. It is a way of life that demands the most exquisite self-examination and a total awareness of what is happening around us.

Tai chi is a form of spiritual exercise, but it can also help to regain the vitality of youth. In the east, health is not just the absence of illness but a philosophy of life. In the practice of tai chi participants seek to find and move their chi through their bodies to maintain and promote their health. The definition of health is the ability that one has to find one's center and thus align oneself with the energy of the universe. A patient is told to cure a disease, find your center, known as the dantien point. It is from this center that a healthy life begins and ends. Given the emphasis on chi force and the meridian map of the body, medicine in the east revolves around a different way of healing. Rather than using proton accelerators and synthetic drugs, eastern doctors use herbal treatments, meditation and massage therapy, acupuncture and external chi gong. All of these methods are designed to restore a healthy flow of chi. They strive to heal the whole body, not just to alleviate the symptoms.

Doctors are very instrumental in this process. They play the role of teacher, guides to their patients in the process of finding their center and moving their chi. The patient/teacher dynamic is critical to recovery: they do not act on their patients, they act with their patients to help them to actively combat their conditions. For example, acupuncture is described as being like fishing in that when the doctor inserts the needle, an interactive process begins between patient and doctor to distinguish between a nibble and a bite. Such methods have been tested through the ages and have been proven to be effective for centuries. Often healing comes through the medium of movement. Movement is more that an enjoyable pastime, it is essential to a healthy life both as prevention and cure. An Eastern saying is that the body is like a hinge on a door: if the body is not "swung open" it will rust.

Exercise 3-8: Being the ball

One of the basic beliefs of eastern philosophers is that experience is essential to understanding. This final exercise requires that you do much more than answer questions:

1. Select any traditional western physical activity (such as tennis) and play the eastern way. (Of course in the case of tennis, this entails much more than adopting the eastern grip, it means that you should seek enlightenment through the traditional approach described above)

2. At your earliest convenience take the opportunity to practice one of the eastern arts (perhaps taichi or aikido) under the watchful and helpful eye of a master

3. Visit a healing practitioner in one of the eastern healing arts (perhaps acupuncture) and engage the healer in a discussion of the philosophy that underlies the practice.

In each case, try to avoid making ethnocentric judgements. Open yourself to alternative ways of being physical and of using physical activity to understand yourself and others.

Review

Understanding others entails reaching beyond a superficial knowledge of what people do and how they live. Understanding involves an element of empathy, a willingness to shed preconceived notions about cultures that are foreign to our experience and a determined effort to walk in the shoes of those being studied. To simply observe and to judge does not lead to understanding as much as it reinforces ethnocentrism. This section has been designed to help you to reach an empathic level of understanding by not only describing the philosophy and practices of eastern culture but by involving you in exercises that help you to experience them. Understanding others helps us to better understand ourselves. Through experiencing the ways of the world, we encounter ourselves. We are challenged to reconsider our own beliefs and patterns of behavior, to adapt our own philosophies of living to new and unexpected cultural norms and to adopt some of the elements that seem more applicable than our old ways of thinking. In this chapter we have explored the eastern tradition, not only as it exists in its homeland, but also as it begins to permeate western society through popular culture and through the practice of medicine and sport. Developing understanding of self and others is a necessary prelude to the next major focus of discussion: living the good life.

Part III

LIVING THE GOOD LIFE

Chapter 4

PLAYING

Preview

In this chapter, you will examine the following aspects of playing:

- the promise of play,

- why people play,

- how play changes as we age,

- the significance of play in your own life,

- the importance of play in the life of a culture.

The Promise of Play

It seems that the deeper we get into the study of movement in kinesiology, the less important play seems to become. It is quite possible that one of the initial attractions of this field of inquiry was its affinity with play. You would not have been alone if you thought as you perused the college catalog, perhaps as a high school senior, that kinesiology sounded like a major in which you could have some fun. Perhaps you thought about the pleasures of your childhood play or the fun of physical activity, and hoped that somehow the study of movement would allow you to revisit this source of personal fulfillment. Instead, you have probably discovered that kinesiology is very serious business. It is as academically rigorous as any other subject matter at the university. It involves the study of the human body and its processes from a range of scholarly perspectives. It requires you to dissect the body, to quantify movement phenomena, to memorize facts and to tussle with theories.

But, rarely do you encounter play. There is good reason for this: it is not easily definable, nor is it quantifiable. Yet, as you well know from your own experience, it is very important. Theorists through the ages have concurred with this view of its significance. For example, Plato, an ancient Greek philosopher whose views have shaped much of western culture, made the assertion that the right way of living is that life must be lived as play. It is no accident that such a considered opinion should be uttered by a prominent philosopher, for philosophy is predominant, among the disciplinary approaches taken to human movement, in it's attempts to shed light on the phenomenon.

Before we can begin to assess the promise of a life lived as play, we must come to grips with the meaning of play. Philosophy can help in this understanding through the process of metaphysical definition to comprehend the nature of the reality of a phenomenon. To understand the nature of the phenomenon of play, we can follow the logical process of distinguishing its essential elements. To further define the nature of play, we can compare and contrast play with associated phenomena to differentiate it from such things as work and sport.

The Elements of Play

Up to this point in your life, play may just be something you do. Perhaps the process of thinking about it would even turn it into something other than play. But before you can get to grips with profound questions of personal and cultural significance, we had better define the nature of play. The following exercise should help to start the process of figuring out what constitutes play in your own experience.

Exercise 4-1: Your childhood play

Think back to the earliest childhood experiences you can recall and describe an activity that you would consider pure play. What were the features of that play experience that strike you as being particularly playful in nature?

Specimen Response: "One early childhood experience that I remember is a form of tag that I call the tree-shadow game. This consisted of running from tree to tree. These were the home bases. Eventually we made the game more complex, and added that only the person who was "it" could be in the sun, everyone else had to remain in the shade and could only run from tree to tree when clouds blocked the sun. Finally, someone introduced blankets into the game as 'sun shields" and the game became a free for all.

There are several playful features exhibited in this experience. It was very amorphous in that the rules and equipment lacked a set form and were always subject to revision. It was self-actuated and individualistic; we determined start and stop times and all the rules and regulations. For the same reasons, imagination and conceptualization are important factors of the experience and often add a fantasy element. Also, the activity was dynamic and uninhibited in the way that we played with "no holds barred" and expended a great amount of energy in our play. Finally, the experience was intrinsically pleasing. We had fun doing it, and so we played."(Chris)

Exercise 4-2. Children at play

As you look around at young people at play, perhaps at your own children, your infant siblings, or perhaps as you visit a kindergarten class, observe their play behavior. What do you consider to be the behavioral common denominators among the children at play that you observe?

Specimen Response: "First the emphasis on formal rules and regulations is minimal. By this, I mean that the structure of the game is not so complicated as to detract from the enjoyment of the game. Second to be fun in some way the activity must be intellectually or physically stimulating. Stimulating is not synonymous with hard. Rather, the activity must be captivating to avoid becoming tedious. Lastly, children partake in the activity for the sake of pure enjoyment and not for ulterior reasons, not because they are forced to do it."(Hilary)

Exercise 4-3. The qualities of play

Make a list of the key features of play as you have experienced and observed it. Also, as we proceed with an analysis of play theory, update and modify this list as you see fit.

Specimen Response: "Key features of play:

- main objective is fun

- no influence from authority

- no outside constraints

- use of imagination

- lack of structure

- play is its own reward"(Ben)

Discussion: I suspect that you had little trouble recognizing play in yourself and in others, but reaching a consensus in definition is more problematic. Playful behavior is distinctive. We can even tell when animals are at play; puppies chase their tails, kittens tease a ball of wool, and lambs frolic in the field. There is a general consensus that underlying playful behavior there are certain defining elements, namely that it is intrinsic, voluntary and has a make-believe quality. The first most generally accepted pillar of play is that it is **intrinsic**. The activity is its own reward. Play is an island of personal integration in a world that is often regulated by externally applied reward and punishment systems. From birth, we learn to seek what we can get out of our actions. At home, toddlers are scolded for their disobedience and treated with candies for good behavior. At school, children are taught to read, write and do their math with an incentive system that ranges from gold stars and who will be door monitor and line leader, to grades and report cards. At work, our very livelihood, benefits and promotions hang on the way we play the game. Only when at play do you indulge yourself in a thoroughly enjoyable activity where the result doesn't really matter.

This element of choice introduces the second generally accepted feature of play, that it is **voluntary**. Play is an expression of your freedom. You choose to play, not because of the fear of retribution, nor to curry favor, but because the action pleases you. Play gives you a sense of control of your own destiny. In this setting, and perhaps in no other, you are freely choosing a course of action, you are responsible for your own behavior and you are in control of the outcomes. At home and at work, you may have to suppress your natural inclinations, but not at play. Play is power. You can temporarily step out of the confines of your daily existence to redefine yourself. Play is a road to self-understanding. Through play you can discover and develop your inner self, because the only constraints you must deal with are those you impose upon yourself.

The third feature of play is its **make-believe** quality. As you enter your play-world, you create your own rules. It has an "as-if" aura. As you observed children at play, you were probably made immediately aware of this quality. They probably took on another persona, assumed different voices and played different roles. Even in your own play, you may have noticed a temporary suspension of reality. As your level of absorption in the activity heightened, you may have become oblivious to your everyday concerns and surroundings. The frustrations and failures of the "real" world temporarily dissipate as you become one with the moment.

Exercise 4-4. Play theory and practice

(handwritten margin note, rotated:) → not tossing frisbee rules; not ultimate w/ playing; not a game, just

How closely did the qualities you identified as essential to play match these three features? At this juncture, you might want to try to translate theory into practice by selecting an activity that you enjoy doing and getting totally involved in it. At its completion, consider the quality of the play experience in light of its intrinsic motivation, the freedom that you felt and expressed and its make-believe nature. Through a process of applied inductive logic, you are approaching an understanding of play.

Specimen Responses: You may choose to respond to this exercise in prose. For example, Ben said, "the qualities I identified as essential to play matched up with the three listed in the chapter (intrinsic, voluntary and make-believe) pretty closely. On Wednesday afternoon, I used an activity I enjoy doing in an attempt to translate the theory into practice. I got totally involved in my evening mountain bike ride and was able to think about its quality as a play experience afterward. As far as my intrinsic motivation in going riding is concerned, it is usually the main reason; being able to use the bike to get outdoors, see interesting things and enjoy the feeling of being on the bike and in control. I used this ride as a fun way to practice bike-handling skills to ride at an easy pace and to enjoy getting away from my training and racing focus for a while.

Being on a bike is a great feeling of freedom. The ability to go virtually anywhere, to see many things, to go extremely fast if I want to and to express myself in my riding style and handling skills are all part of the freedom that a mountain bike, or road bike, bring me. The ride I went on was a perfect expression of freedom; it was a new trail to explore, it was just me, my bike and the woods, and I was able to ride exactly how I felt.

As far as the make-believe component of my ride, I really didn't make things up. I just enjoyed the flow of how things were happening naturally and as they came up. Sometimes I pretend that I am a pro rider hammering on the road or trail."

Alternatively, you may decide to be more graphic in your comparison. Chris shows how the features of play that he identified in his own activities contrast with the qualities discussed in the previous section in the following table:

Intrinsic	Voluntary	Make believe	
•		•	amorphous
	•		self-actuated
•			individualistic
•		•	imagination
•			conceptualization
	•		fantasy element
•	•		dynamic
•	•		uninhibited
•	•		intrinsically pleasing
•			true expression

He proceeds to explain that, "the X's above indicate how the play attributes that I have listed line up with the three defining elements of play, that it should have intrinsic, voluntary and make-believe qualities. In order to test these qualities, I played the wonderfully addictive game of Tetris on the computer. There is a certain smug satisfaction each time you complete a row and make the blocks disappear. This alone is enough to intrinsically motivate the player and to make it fun. I willingly found myself playing again and again, and I quickly lost track of time. Also, a fantasy quality exists in the concept that these blocks are falling from the sky and you alone can manipulate them and order them and happily do it for no clearly defined goal. The relative quality of the play experience was quite high. It was inherently fun. It was of my own volition. I became completely self-absorbed while playing."

Play As Not-Work

Another way of defining phenomena is through contrast. Work and play are a commonly understood dichotomy. They are generally considered to be mutually exclusive when used in such sayings as, "all work and no play makes Jack a dull boy." Play is thought to be a counterpoint, even an antidote, to the rigors of work. Juxtaposing the criteria of play already discussed into the equation, it is easy to see why. Unlike play, work is characterized by its extrinsic motivation, by a loss of personal control and by an inescapable reality. Work is something you do for reasons beyond the activity itself. At school, you work to get grades, to graduate and then to get a job. Once you have the job, you work to pay the bills, to feed and clothe yourself and your dependents, to earn enough to be able to play. Play is what you do because its fun, work is often what you do in order to have fun. Play comes from your own volition. It is often spontaneous, something you do on the spur of the moment because it feels good. In contrast, work is forced upon you. It is a daily necessity in order to survive and thrive. That element of compulsion often creates a sense of personal alienation because you don't feel that you control your own existence. The loss of choice implies loss of control. Play is empowering because you are able to decide your own course of action, whereas at work you are often at the beck and call of your superiors, subject to the whims of your peers and at the mercy of the market. The spontaneity of play can be transposed against the routine of work.

Time governs your workday. You must arrive at a specified hour, complete tasks on schedule and punch the clock when you leave. In fact, time can seem to be your worst enemy, as you hurry to do everything demanded of you when there don't seem to be enough hours in the day. Stress and hurry-sickness are symptomatic of a workplace out of your control. As you rush from one assigned task to the next, it is natural to yearn for relaxation, for a time when you can set your own agenda, for play. Work can be impersonal. You can be treated as a cog in a machine, as part of the production process. You are expected to behave and to dress in a certain way. You must conform to company rules and regulations if you want to get ahead. You even assume a false identity in some work settings to mask your inner sensibilities and to hide your sensitive vulnerable inner being, or to act in ways that seem false or forced and even to ignore your own best judgement. In such settings, you inevitably feel like a round peg in a square hole.

Only away from this alienating context can you let your hair down, be yourself and play. As you play, time flies. You can become totally absorbed in an activity, minutes can merge into hours, you can enter a state of flow. Your self-consciousness and your behavior converge to the point that you are oblivious to your surroundings, to the trials and tribulations of daily life and to the passage of time. Watching the clock at work, a day can seem to be an eternity. There is no make-believe quality, no suspension of reality, in a work setting that you find alienating and coercive.

Of course, life is not so black and white. The act of work can assume playful qualities and play can become quite serious. Work does not have to be alienating. Many people find a career in which they can blend their skills and their interests. It can be an enjoyable, satisfying marriage of personal talents and financial opportunity. Such fortunate individuals may be heard to claim that they would choose to do their work even if they were not paid for their efforts. They have fun at work, they choose to do what they do and they can become completely absorbed in a project.

They are truly following Plato's advice that, life must be lived as play. The conclusion that we can draw from this apparent anomaly is that it is not the act itself, but the quality of the specific act, that is the distinguishing feature. An attitude of playfulness may pervade the process of work. It is this attitude that gives play its distinctive quality.

Exercise 4-5: Work and play

Experience the contrast to understand the distinction between work and play. Attitude has been identified as the key defining ingredient and your attitude is something you have some control over. Try approaching activities that you would have previously identified as work and as play with the following criteria in mind: intrinsic/extrinsic worth, freedom of choice/coercion of effort and absorption/ alienation in mind. Of course, it is not possible to make something you totally hate into play, nor is it easy to work at eating ice cream. Nevertheless, you will be able to find many activities that span the gulf between the two extremes.

Specimen Response: "I experimented with my attitude to define the difference between play and work for myself. I usually "work" when I lift weights hence I tried to develop a plan to view this activity as play. I thought of how I could release my hostility towards one of my classmates (in accounting class) by participating in a weight session. I also invited a friend to join me and was content with my freedom of choice in the situation. My workout was highly enjoyable as a result of changing my perspective and incorporating elements of play into the activity

I considered my run yesterday to be work. I incurred a stress fracture last spring and although it has healed, I am forced to run on the track at times (for added cushioning). The monotony of the experience robbed the voluntary aspect of play from my activity. The feeling of intrinsic work that I normally possess when I run was absent from the experience because I found the activity boring. I had to prevent myself from using the make-believe element of play to imagine myself on a wooded running trail. I concluded that I would much rather make work play than play work."(Melissa)

Play and Sport

Another approach to the discovery of meaning is through comparison. Play and sport may have seemed to be synonymous until now, and, indeed, it is possible and perhaps even usual for you to "play" a sport. But, sport can also adopt the face of work. When athletes don't enjoy the activity itself but participate for external rewards, a sport that was probably once play for them becomes work. They may be doing it for the financial gain of a salary or a scholarship, the prestige of fame, popularity among their peers, the muscular lean look, the fitness that accrues from the exertion or the health and longevity associated with exercise. But, when they are not doing it because they enjoy it, the playfulness dissipates.

Similarly, sport can be something you turn to as a natural outlet for your playful urges. Sport and youthfulness are a perfect match; they are both physical in nature and both have boundless horizons and promise. Yet, play does not always result from their union. Too often, the possibilities of sport are compromised by curtailment of personal freedom. Athletes may enter into sport of their own volition, although in the case of many college and professional athletes they may also feel obliged to be there because they are being paid for their services.

In the case of organized sport, athletes are often confronted with a minefield of rules and regulations that may severely curtail their liberty to participate as they choose. The more they are subjected to a coercive system, the less play-like sport seems. It is the nature of sport to have boundaries. The rules of the game are their defining element. They are essential to sports participation and generally do not in themselves constrain play. However they do tend to eliminate such playful acts as those of William Webb Ellis, a high school student at Rugby School in England, who is reputed to have decided to pick the ball up and run with it during a soccer game, and thus invented rugby. In most cases, players are happy to play within the limits set by the rules of the game. Indeed, it is these very rules that attracted them to the activity in the first place.

The coercion that constrains their freedom and lessens their ability to play derives from other sources, most particularly from coaches. The higher the stakes of winning, the more serious an affair sport becomes for coaches. Often, their livelihood depends upon their win/loss record. There is no time for fun and games when just one false move may be the difference between victory and defeat. The job of the coach is too often to instill discipline into the athletes, and in the process remove the spontaneity, the individuality and the joy. "It's my way or the highway" is the clarion call of such coaches as they impose their will on their teams. They demand that players move when and how they say on the field or court and that they follow the team rules in every respect. This blind obedience frequently applies to matters of personal taste, such as rules which legislate what athletes should eat, drink and wear, who they should hang out with, their sleep and study habits and their personal conduct. In such a regimented environment, an athlete dare not be playful. To do so would be to jeopardize access to the activity that has been so meaningful in the past as a source of self-knowledge, self-esteem and fun. Athletes may still be able to become immersed in the activity, so totally engrossed that time and space merge into a sense of flow, but in organized sports the coach has a tendency to bring them back to the reality of "big-time sports" in a hurry. Athletes may often do their sport because they want to, but dealing with the dictates of an authority figure can make them wish they were somewhere else. Athletes can genuinely enjoy their sporting experience, but the emphasis on extrinsic gratification can detract from the playfulness of participation. It is possible to play in sport but sport can also become a form of work. It can be restricted by routines, product-oriented and depersonalized.

Exercise 4-6: Sport and play

Think of and list situations in your own experience when sport has felt more like work than play. Describe the relationship of play and work in these cases by answering the following questions. A specimen response is provided to help guide your thinking.

Question: How are the qualities of play important to you?

Specimen Response: "the qualities of play are what make sport appealing in the first place. It is intrinsic, free, make-believe. When the sports become "games of limitation" with rules, boundaries and so on, they lose their original focus as an outlet for play."

Question: In what ways do major sports not measure up to these criteria?

Specimen Response: "The limiting qualities of major sports is that they stifle the playful qualities. The presence of referees and other officials negates intrinsic values, lines and boundaries preclude freedom and the make-believe, fantasy quality is lost to rules and regulations and statistics."

Question: What are your feelings on the matter?

Specimen Response: "It seems that play and sport have a common ancestry, but are by no means genetic clones. It appears that play and sport are not a dichotomy, but an evolutionary continuum in the cultural life of a society. Play is born from the needs for fantasy, self-expression and freedom of movement. Sport evolves from play but satisfies other human needs. Rules and statistics quench our thirst for competition. Regulations provide us with challenges to overcome within set parameters and hone our tactical and strategic thinking skills."

As a postscript to this discussion of the meaning of play, it is important to recognize that play is a dynamic, ever-changing aspect of living. As a form of play becomes popular it tends to become more structured. It seems to be an innate quality of human nature to want to control and shape every aspect of living including the games we play. Activities that start as play tend to become structured into sports. For example, from the playful counter culture game of frisbee that was played purely for fun and recreation in the decade of the 1960s grew the sport of ultimate frisbee. An exercise in freedom matured into a highly competitive team event replete with rules and regulations that prescribe and restrict participatory behavior. The paradox is that the more we impose the structures and strictures of work on our play activities, the less playful they tend to become.

Review and Preview

To summarize the previous discussion, a playful attitude is the essential defining quality of play. This attitude is premised upon the criteria of intrinsic motivation, freedom of choice and suspension of reality. It is evident from the preceding discussion that play is a subjective and idiosyncratic form of human expression. One person's delight is another person's poison. Play has an ephemeral quality. What starts as play may become a chore, or, alternatively, the most arduous tasks may assume play-like proportions. Although it is often linked with sport, physical activity, recreation and leisure, play is ubiquitous and universal. It can take place at work, doing household chores, in activities that are predominantly cerebral, even in the process of daydreaming. It is the most unique, diverse and creative expression of human being.

So far in this chapter we have been engaged in the process of defining play through it's constituents and through contrast. We have identified qualities that are generally associated with play and have compared play with work and sport. We can conclude that play is both action and attitude, an enjoyable experience undertaken in a playful spirit.

Now we will consider purpose. Why do people play and how does that process change as we age? Plato suggested that life must be lived as play. Does this mandate still apply to you today? Should it be a cultural imperative?

Why People Play

You are by now familiar enough with the ways of philosophy to appreciate that philosophers are always asking, "what do you mean by?" and "why?" So far in this section we have been responding to the question, "what do you mean by play?" Now we will turn our attention to examining why people play, and more specifically, what motivates your own play behaviors. People seek a multiplicity of meanings in and through play. No two people are the same, nor are their goals, aspirations or actions identical. Yet, through the ages play has been a constant; something everybody does and that everyone seems to want to do more. Early theorists suggested several explanations for why people play. The instinct, recapitulation, preparation, learning, developmental, and surplus energy theories may be pieces of the puzzle, but they all have shortcomings too.

Perhaps, as early theorists speculated, play is an **instinct**. Children play for much the same reason as mothers protect their young: because they have no choice. It is part of the human blueprint. A deep-seated urge wells up from our inner being. We play because we must, because it is virtually part of our genetic code. Instinct theory has come under fire by critics who question whether such things as inherited unlearned capacities to act even exist. They have suggested that we are not created as a preformed package complete with a range of instincts, but that we evolve through our learned responses to our environment.

Another explanation that resembles the instinct rationale in certain basic ways, is that play is a form of **recapitulation**. Like instinct theory, this approach presumes that we are born with certain innate encoded tendencies. Having observed the progression of play patterns from the stages of warrior to worker, from survival to service and from conquest to community, play theorists have recognized a resemblance to the history of the development of the species. Perhaps, they speculate, these critical behaviors are encoded for inheritance and we emit them in a play setting because they are no longer essential in the "real" world. Watching little children progress from the hitting stage to cooperative play, from playing alone to playing in groups and from self centered to social play you might see the evolution of the species. It may be possible to read into sports and games elements of hunting, chasing and fighting which seem to mirror the development of the human race. Once again, the explanatory power of the theory rests on a Darwinian concept of a clear line of evolution that is not acceptable to many modern theorists.

Another theory that relates play to personal progress is the **preparation** theory that holds that play is the effort of the player to prepare for later life. Certainly, as you watch little Kendra playing at house or with her Barbie, or young Sean playing with his fire engine, you may sense that these actions have real world connotations: that play is rehearsal. Children may be mimicking adults around them, or they may be instinctively prepared for responses that will be important in their later lives. In either case, youth is the period during which these inherited propensities are refined.

In marked contrast to the group of theories that are premised upon the existence of inherited instinct, **learning** and **developmental** theories posit explanations that depend upon the interaction of individuals with their environments. Learning theory is a behaviorist paradigm, which suggests that play is caused by the normal stimulus-response processes that stimulate learning. In other words, children act in ways that will produce pleasant effects and avoid negative consequences, which entails selecting play activities that make them feel good. Similarly, developmental theory focuses less on innate characteristics than upon growth and personal development. Basically, children will play at the level appropriate for their maturation process. As their intellect develops and their ability to impose conceptions and constraints on their actions grows they will become bored with the games that used to hold their attention and will seek out more challenging pastimes.

As persuasive as each of these theories may be as explanations of why children play, they do not begin to provide reasons for adult play. Although play may still be instinctive in our later years, it would be hard to argue that there is much recapitulation or preparation going on in adult play. The **surplus energy** theory may have more explanatory power here. This holds that we generate and store a particular quantity of energy to meet the needs of daily living and that we often have some left over. This is when we "blow off steam". Play is a healthy vent for negative energy that can cause disruption and discomfort.

Another traditional explanation of why we play is because of our need for **relaxation**. It seems plausible that we need to emit responses other than those used in work to facilitate our recuperation from the rigors of our jobs and that through relaxation we can purge ourselves of the noxious byproducts of work. It does not, however explain the use in play of activities also used in work, nor does it help us to understand the play of those who are out-of-work or of children who are not yet at work.

More recent theories redress these imbalances by relating play patterns to work outcomes. **Generalization** theory suggests that people will seek out experiences in play that have been rewarding at work. For example, if you are an ambitious loner in the office, you might gravitate towards individual play activities that provide the opportunity of getting ahead [golf comes to mind]. Conversely, **compensation** theory proposes that people play in order to fulfil psychic needs not satisfied at work. Because you are a loner at work who has the reputation of climbing over your colleagues backs to get to the top, you crave play experiences that are social in nature, perhaps the result doesn't even matter. Rather than play a cutthroat game of tennis, you opt for synchronized swimming.

Catharsis theory takes the idea of compensation one step further. It explains play as an avenue down which the player can express disorganizing emotions in a harmless way in socially sanctioned activities. Aggression, which may be generated in other spheres of life can either be expressed in violent confrontation or can be purged through vigorous physical activity, proponents of this position contend. Better to hurl yourself into a tackle than a fellow worker. However critics of catharsis theory question whether expression of hostility in any setting can purge feelings of aggression. Furthermore, violent conduct in play may have the opposite of the desired effect; it may increase rather than decrease hostility and aggression.

Finally, **psychoanalytic** theories of play focus on the adjustment of people at play to feelings engendered elsewhere. On the one hand players may repeat in a playful form strongly unpleasant experiences thereby reducing their seriousness and facilitating their assimilation. On the other, players may reverse the role of passive recipient of unpleasant treatment by actively manipulating and mastering an opponent at play. If you feel like a whipping boy at the office, it may be gratifying to dominate someone in sport, particularly if you can get the same malevolent boss to play against you!

Exercise 4-7: Why do you play?

Now here comes the hard part; determining your own motivation. Ask yourself which of these explanatory theories seems most plausible. Bear in mind that they are not necessarily mutually exclusive. If several theories ring true for you, assign them valencies to indicate relative plausibility. Then, as always in this applied approach to philosophy, test out your assessment on the playing field. During a period of time complete a number of play experiences and as you do so, consciously evaluate why you are playing. In each case use these theories as your criteria of assessment by assigning a numerical weight to each theory on each occasion [from 1=highly influential to 5= not at all]. Here is a table that will allow you to record nine play experiences (you may find that you don't need to complete all nine to reach your conclusion):

Instinct									
Recapitulation									
Preparation									
Surplus Energy									
Relaxation									
Developmental									
Learning									
Generalization									
Compensation									
Catharsis									
Psychoanalytic									
Total points:									

Discussion: When you have completed your play activities and recorded your scores on this table, tally the numbers across each row. The lower the number, the greater the explanatory power of the play theory in your case. As you think about the relative relevance of these theories to your play, you can draw certain conclusions about the meaning of play in your life. As an example, Melissa conducted the following self-evaluation; "After completing the play exercises, I conclude that I play for the purpose of relaxation the majority of the time. Secondly, I play to release my surplus energy. Most of the play activities that I engage in do not conform to the preparation theory because I am no longer a child. However, it could be argued that a chess match promotes the acquisition of military strategy essential for warfare, which I am prepping myself for. I found that the activities that I enjoyed most were usually instinctual. I did not have to worry about providing the correct answer for a question, or being certain that my canoeing paddle entered the water smoothly. I favored activities that came naturally to me because I could free my mind to wander. I also love the discipline that it takes to go for a long run most days or ride the stationary bike. It requires a certain degree of the effort that I bring to the class-room. I realize that this reasoning falls into the generalization theory in which people seek out experiences at play which have rewarded them in the workplace. When I play, it is to please myself. I don't have to worry about the time, or my surroundings. I am free to absorb an intrinsic peace without guilt. I can be whatever or whomever I want."

Play As You Grow

Play is a universal condition that spans the generations. Consider the small child playing with a set of building blocks. The child develops coordination, proprioception, a sense of touch and a host of other abilities through play. In addition, the same child recognizes an ability to affect the environment, to build and to destroy towers of the imagination. Through play the child takes the first tentative steps away from mother towards independence. As we grow older, our perceptions of play, our reasons for playing and the way we play all change, but they don't disappear. Sadly, perhaps, one of the measures of maturity in our culture is the ability to hide our real selves. As we develop our adult identities, genuine expressions of spontaneity tend to become submerged under a veneer of sophistication. Consequently, a game that might have been a simple expression of exuberance and energy in childhood can adopt various subliminal undertones when played by the adult. It might become a game of power and dominance, a sexual encounter or a vehicle for psychological warfare or introspective reflection.

During the aging process, the games people play tend to focus upon the psychology of human relationships. Play may be an exploitative manipulation or social stroking behavior. Perhaps you approach the tennis court determined to dominate and demolish your opponent, or maybe you enter the same game with the expectation of mutual accord. Every ball hit may be a threat, a challenge or even an insult; in effect a sanctioned form of fighting. Alternatively, each rally could be a harmonious dialogue punctuated by mutual admiration and support. Similarly, solitary pastimes serve an array of psychological functions for the adult.

The last exercise you did asked you to focus on motivational theories. What were your conclusions? It might clarify the theoretical basis of your own play choices if you more closely assess the type of activity you tend to gravitate towards. Perhaps you crave health and fitness for functional reasons: to live longer, to look better, to feel better. If you are one of those intrepid characters who chooses to rappel from high places, challenge troubled waters in flimsy crafts or hurtle through the air at great speed, you are probably a thrill seeker. One who enjoys taking risks, who seeks out extreme sensory stimulation, who relishes the pursuit of vertigo. By choosing group activities ranging from disco dancing to team sports for social reasons you may fulfill affiliative needs for social approval, status, acceptance and love. To satiate your aesthetic sensibilities, you might turn to activities which stress appreciation of beauty in form, ranging from creative arts, like sculpture, to kinesthetic pastimes, like creative movement, gymnastics and diving. You may play to escape from guilt and anxiety, to find security or just to relax. There are even those who play for ascetic reasons of self-denial and curiously, find pleasure in mid-winter swimming.

Whatever you typically choose to play, it is inevitable that the innocent naivete of your youthful play has been replaced by a network of adult drives and desires during the metamorphosis of maturation. As we age, we change. The rich fantasy world of our youth takes on new dimensions. Formalized sports take the place of make-believe play. The interplay between our growth and our play reflects the evolution of needs and competencies necessary to survive and flourish in modern society. Children play, in part, to discover themselves, to experiment with different roles and characters, to develop an identity. As they mature, the security of the family is replaced by the uncertainties of self-sufficiency. One value of play for these emerging adults is that they can temporarily control their environment. Activities selected may allow them to compensate for inadequacies at home and failures at work. They provide the opportunity to experience the sense of mastery and competence lacking in other spheres of life. As children grow up, their world becomes increasingly complex and confusing, daily decisions are more time-consuming, complicated and threatening. In a world beyond our control, in which we are being forced to absorb more and more information, often of a complex, technical nature, at an increasingly accelerated rate, play is a comforting medium of mastery. One of the attractions of such burgeoning activities as jogging and mountain biking is that they give people of all ages and all physical conditions an opportunity to be successful, however slowly or awkwardly they may move.

As we change through the aging process, so the world in which we live changes. The demands of family and work, of education and worship tend to curb the creativity of our childhood. Where children can dream and create personal play worlds, adults generally need structure. The child may play. The adult must play at something, usually a game. Perhaps because we learn that organization and structure are vital for survival at home and work, the majority of adults choose play activities that are hedged in by rules and regulations. In the major sports of this country, the flow of the game is legislated, and deviations from that pattern are eliminated by a complex code of behavior. It simply is not acceptable to kick the basketball, continue playing football beyond the sidelines of the field or to use two pitchers simultaneously in baseball. It seems that the more statistics dominate and the more goal-oriented the sporting activity becomes, the less spontaneity we see in the participants. As a sport develops, it becomes less playful in nature. A sport, like a child, tends to be most playful when young.

Without a moment of playfulness, sports would not have been conceived. For example, James Naismith was giving his creative energies full rein as he played with some peach baskets to conjure up the game of basketball. Even strategical and technical innovations in a sport may be credited as much to the playful spirit of mankind as to the marvels of technological research. Whoever first grasped the tennis racket with two hands forever changed the game, and whoever inspired Dick Fosbury with the notion of vaulting stomach up revolutionized the high jump. But these playful pioneers are few; most people prefer to conform to the structure of sport and to model their skills after a predefined style, even when that entails trying to insert a square peg into a round hole. The hole is an idealized image of how to perform. The square peg is that uncooperative body. The danger is that in the process of trying to be successful, we forget to "play" the game.

Rather, adults tend to adopt a medical model of remediation, like a patient working to recover from some benign disease. Does this analogy resonate with your own experience of performance enhancement? The first step toward getting better is to select an "expert" to diagnose your problem: a technique therapist. During a session, this expert prescribes a series of practices to remedy the flaws in your game. Then comes the arduous system of rehabilitation consisting of practice, drills and occasional follow-up checkups. Occasionally, you can see the system working, thanks to application, dedication and perceptive instruction which is just enough to give hope and spur you to extra effort. But, unless you are among the fortunate few, those hours of practice may still have left you with some unnatural and inefficient movements. People react differently to the frustrations of failure. Some are spurred by their shortcomings to try and try again until they fit that final piece into the movement jigsaw. But, most react with anger and eventually withdrawal to such problems; rackets find their way over the fence and eventually back to the closet. Attempts to remedy deficiencies in a game have failed; the malaise seems terminal.

Play has become work. The healthy uplifting features of play have given way to frustration and failure. The emphases on correct technique, on the accumulation of points and on statistical perfection have eclipsed the joy of doing, the freedom of expression and the make-believe qualities of play. The unique athlete struggling to express itself within each one of us is necessarily stifled by such a system. Conformity and uniformity are not the only lessons we learn at work and apply to play. In much of our "leisure" activity, no less than in our work activity, we place a high value on advanced planning and goal setting and on competition and winning. We gain promotions at work and improve performance in sport through mastering progressively specialized knowledge and techniques. In the office and on the basketball court we stress the efficient utilization of time. What would the modern game of basketball be without the tension with time illustrated by the three-second rule, the shot clock and time-outs? As the strictures of maturity and the structures of work infiltrate play, we seem to lose the ability to dream and create, to suspend time and reality.

Exercise 4-8: Playing and Aging

Discuss your own play progression and how the emphasis on each of the following topics has changed through the years:

- uniformity
- conformity
- advanced planning
- goal-setting
- competition
- winning
- specialization
- time-management
- correct technique

Exercise 4-9: Reliving your childhood play

Another exercise that can be illuminating is to try to play as a child once again by minimizing each of the qualities listed above as you focus on the intrinsic, liberating, creative qualities of the experience. Through experiencing the complications of stepping back in time to your youth you will appreciate the effects of maturation on play habits.

Specimen response: "It took me a while to decide what to do, but finally I decided to go to the playground. I have to admit it was a lot more fun than I thought it was going to be. No one else wanted to join me so I had to play by myself. That took a little bit away from the fun, but it truly was liberating to leave my inhibitions and discretion behind and act like a ten year old kid again. I did it all, from the swings, to the sandpit, to the wooden structures. It was invigorating and it made me reflect on the innocence of childhood and forget about my upcoming test and this project and work for a while. That was the best part about the day, I didn't think of all the responsibilities which I had hanging over my head. Even though I didn't plan on it, this was probably my favorite play experience because of its liberating qualities."

Why Live Your Life As Play?

At first glance, the notion of living life as play may seem too fanciful. How can anyone shirk the responsibilities of everyday life and of work? This question is certainly very reasonable, but it assumes that play is a form of hedonistic self-gratification, where in fact play may embrace both responsibility and remuneration, both employment and effort. Play is more than self-indulgence. It is living life according to your own rules, but not at the expense of your potential. Because of its innate value, play may enhance your productivity, allowing you to blossom as a person. This value may be measured first in terms of **personal freedom.**

Play is freedom from falseness and the tyranny of work and freedom to pursue an authentic lifestyle. In one sense, then, it is a form of escape from a mode of being that is forced upon you by the dictates of society. Too often, people find work that is not pleasing to them. They then fall into a way of life that is draining, stressful and boring. Time marches inexorably on while they remain trapped in their self-assumed prison. Perhaps they dream of the pleasures that their work will pay for on their vacations, or after retirement. They endure the pain of work to enjoy the pleasure of play. The grim reality of work is that it can take the best years of your life and only give in return rewards and benefits external to it.

When Plato admonished that life should be lived as play, he was not only referring to the moments of leisure time that exist apart from work, but to the whole of life. To interpret this idea two thousand years later in the context of modern society, you should choose to do in life things that make you happy. Plato was not advocating hedonistic self-indulgence, but rather that we should treat work and leisure as a venue for self-discovery and self-fulfillment. Play does not imply lack of effort. Indeed, it is when at play that people tend to expend most effort because they want to be doing what they are doing. But, it does imply an element of choice and an effort to discover what will make you happy and what particular forms of employment may entail.

Choice without understanding, like freedom without purpose, can become anarchy. To avoid such personal disintegration, work choices should be part of the philosophic process of reacting, self-distancing, identifying, analyzing and synthesizing described in the introductory chapter. To make the most playful choice of occupation, avoid the temptation of reacting to your pecuniary needs by snatching at the first reasonably paid job that comes along. Instead, step back from the situation to identify what makes you happy and what opportunities the range of vocations available to you might offer to meet your happiness criteria. This entails self analysis and job research. Synthesizing your own needs and the opportunities afforded by your employment options will maximize the possibility of play at work. By so doing, you may escape the yoke of work. Instead of spending hours of drudgery earning the wherewithal to enjoy your leisure time, work and play can be unified. You can reap rewards in, not just from, your work. Instead of putting on your work face every morning as you reluctantly enter your place of employment you can be authentic. You are not acting in bad faith, donning the ill-fitting mask of a disgruntled worker but can approach each day as a player in that you are doing a satisfying task of your own volition.

A second value of living life as play is that it brings **personal unity**. At play, you are at one with yourself. Children don't compartmentalize themselves into mind\body\spirit. Such disintegration is a product of a western upbringing. We tend to lose touch with the connectedness of our inner being, to fragment our language, thoughts and actions. Only when at play do we begin to approach a re-unification of ourselves as we become absorbed and engrossed by a particular activity. Only then do we really heed our physiological discourse. Although our bodies are constantly trying to call attention to our needs, we only respond to the most desperate cries of hunger or the need to expel. At play, we listen attentively. By living an artificial existence, by fabricating an imposed lifestyle and by forcing ourselves to work in frustrating and unfulfilling jobs, we create internal stress and "dis-ease". But at play, our bodies, minds and spirits are in sync to the point that they are indivisible. As our bodies speak, we listen. When our bodies hurt, we slow down. As our intensity rises, our bodies respond by approaching their potential. We are at one with our biorhythms. There is no internal disjunction, no distress beyond that which we willingly impose on ourselves. Such personal unity, at work and during leisure is vital to your health and wellbeing.

Play represents **personal possibility**. Through play we confirm our being and affirm our unique value. At no other time do you feel more alive than when you are totally into something you really want to do. You may be expressing yourself in familiar ways or discovering novel avenues of creativity as you play. Through such self-expression and self-discovery you explore and confirm the parameters of your existence: who you are and who you can be. We are all unique so we all play in different ways. For example, you may play through sport or speech, through poetry or painting at home or at work. It is precisely this idiosyncratic quality of what and how you play that allows you to affirm your unique value. No one else approaches life exactly as you do. By testing your own limits in your own way, you realize the qualities that are yours, and yours alone. Through play you can encounter the world of wonder, the joy of existence and the anguish of failure. You can reach a realm of being beyond that accessible through a humdrum existence. It is an opportunity to imagine, to spread your wings and fly, to become. Life must be lived as play because it is the avenue down which you can reach your potential. In the same way that you cannot have a dream come true if you don't have a dream, you cannot become all that you can be if you don't play. Through play one can find the genesis of self-creation and the evolution of self-actualization.

Play is a form of **personal re-creation**. Through play you can go forwards by moving backwards. We can strip away layers of sophistication by rediscovering the innocence of youth. Through play we can become more childlike. Childlike, not in the sense of throwing tantrums, pouting and pulling hair, but in such qualities as idealized perspectives, unbridled enthusiasm and total commitment. Instead of becoming gnarled and calloused by the vicissitudes of life, we can seek regeneration through play. It is a thread that can run through our lives, connecting us today with the experiences and mindset of yesterday. Like a fountain of youth, you can sip the playfulness you once knew to taste those qualities you wish to recreate in yourself. It is unlikely that you would select the same activity to play at the age of twenty five or fifty five that you played when you were five, but it may be possible to get in touch once again with the attitudes you once embraced. The manipulative mind games of domination that tend to epitomize the adult world may be supplanted by cooperative, imaginative interactive play. Perhaps you can rekindle the awe and bright-eyed curiosity of the children first encountering their world. Through play, the child lurking within each one of us can be freed to rejuvenate and recreate our lived experience, to help us appreciate the beauty in life and to rekindle optimism.

Ultimately, play is a primary source of **personal happiness**. It can be freeing, fulfilling, affirming and transcending. It is always fun. When it ceases to be a source of pleasure, it ceases to be play. The rewards of play are manifold and reach into all dimensions of our existence. To use the dualistic language of dichotomy with which we communicate in the western world, play contributes to physical, psychological, emotional, social and spiritual wellbeing. We derive happiness from achieving a sense of wellbeing by freely doing that which we find pleasurable. In play we celebrate life and revel in the moment of our own existence.

The following exercises are designed to help you to further understand why life should be lived as play.

Exercise 4-10: Why should life be lived as play?

Take each of these values of play and try to identify how freedom, unity, possibility, recreation and happiness have accrued from your own play experiences.

Specimen Response: Chris recognized each of these play outcomes in his own experiences: "freedom accrues from any activity that is performed voluntarily. It is further evidenced in activities that extend the consciousness outside of the body. Sailing and singing are two things that do this for me. In each case I feel that I become part of something greater than my self, and this is very freeing. Any activity in which you are able to get "in the zone" can have the same effect.

When an activity requires your all, you achieve unity of mind, body and spirit because there is no other choice. This unity is natural and so we can easily fall back into it during play. There are some activities that help to promote unity all the time, through an internalizing, contemplative approach to self. Tai chi is an example. Another that is one of my favorites is yoga. These arts require slowing down and listening to the body, calming the mind and nourishing the spirit.

Dance is the activity that comes to mind when I think of personal possibility. This past year I had the opportunity to be in the cast of *42nd St.* and we worked many long hours on both tap and jazz dance routines. One evening close to opening night, the director/choreographer spoke to us about dancing. She said that whether we knew it or not, we were now dancers. We may not have been before this show, but we were now, and we were good. This was an amazing revelation to me and a moment of self-discovery. I had never thought of myself as a dancer before, but now I was.

One of the reasons that people love children so much is that they provide an ample opportunity for recreating our youthful play experiences. We find that it is acceptable to get down on the floor with kids and play with children's toys. We are able to get in touch with the naivete of their play experiences and can play vicariously through them.

One of the easiest ways to make work into play is to find things that impart happiness. If you love your career, the most likely reason is that it, or certain aspects of it, make you happy. One of my favorite pastimes is reading and I love to learn new things so I find that school is a lot like play for me."

Exercise 4-11: The problems of play

Be a "devil's advocate." The description of the values of play that we have adopted so far is Aristotelian. It assumes the basic goodness of human nature, which means that everyone will tend to gravitate towards a higher good when given the opportunity and freedom to play. Take the position of an opposing camp of theorists, who suggest that liberty leads to license, that people left to their own devices will get up to mischief and will satiate their own selfish appetites at the expense of others. What then are the values of play (if any)? Given this context, should life still be lived as play?

Specimen Responses: This struck a responsive chord in Melissa, who recalled vivid memories, "I understand the darker side of play. I remember boys in my elementary school class experimented with aerosol can bombs and mutilated the squirrels that they found on the side of the road. The novel *Lord of the Flies* is a perfect example of play diverting to mischief and chaos." She concluded that, "a certain order should accompany play or else there is no enjoyment to be derived from it. Rules and regulations can increase the challenges and rewards of play."

Hilary was concerned that, "people will always challenge the boundaries to assert their individuality."

Michael suggested that socialization and the maturation process tend to eliminate the darker sides of play. "This concept is one which is very interesting and intriguing to me. The way I think of it, everyone at one point in their lives has lost their temper while playing. This is illustrated in things such as fights in games and on the schoolyard. If someone hurts you while you are playing in a game, the first thing you want to do is to get revenge and attempt to hurt them. The values of play in this context would be aggression, revenge, rage and anger. Does this mean that we should stop living life as play? No, because this is such a small part of play and as you get older it happens less and less. Playing is one of the few harmless releases that we as humans have and retain. It is positive 99% of the time with very few exceptions."

This exercise may make us realize that play is not necessarily a panacea for all of our problems. In some cases, play may become mischief. It may be a destructive force, a means of manipulation and exploitation. But, overall play is like sunshine. It can cause discomfort (sunburn) and even death (skin cancer), but it will more frequently bring light and warmth to our existence.

Why Live A Culture's Life As Play?

The importance of play in the life of a culture is indicated by the conditions in the United States at the turn of this century. American society faces a plague of social problems such as increasing dependency (as in escalating drug use), death rates (homicide, that is) and despair (evidenced in acute depression and a soaring suicide rate). Many Americans are bewildered by the rapid rate of change. They are not part of the computer culture and feel out of the information loop. Many can't even program their VCR! In short, they feel isolated, alienated and threatened. They do not feel in control of their lives.

Play is one means of regaining a semblance of control, albeit only temporarily. Paradoxically, advances in technology have increased our control of the normal living environment. Air conditioning and central heating have created a thermostat-controlled home, at every turn we are faced with creature comforts. Risks and challenges have been minimized. Play can reintroduce an element of risk into the life of an individual who is bored by the monotony of living in an antiseptic, climate-controlled world. The boom in risk activities in the great outdoors, such as whitewater rafting, canoeing and kayaking, spelunking, rock-climbing and rapelling and boardsailing, are a testament to the thirst for adventure that is not being quenched in everyday life but that can be satisfied through play.

Play is a positive force in every realm of a culture's life. From worship to work, a society is more vibrant when it adopts a play ethic. Without a playful spirit religion can be a repetitive liturgy, a Sunday spent being preached at, a weekly ritual devoid of significance. Infused with play, religion can become a search for personal meaning in an impersonal world. Elements of play, such as creativity, spontaneity, and a willingness to suspend daily reality can transform a boring habit into a spiritual quest. Fully entering into the sacred rituals of religion engages the worshiper in a process of pure play. Intrinsic to most church liturgy is a leap of faith, a willingness to step beyond the world of reason to seek meaning in mythology. The qualities of the religious experience, then, are the same as those that define play: a suspension of reality and a willingness to seek the inner goods in an activity freely chosen.

Similarly, at work the most mundane task can become gratifying when approached as play. Recognizing this factor, many forward-looking employers are changing their work-sites to incorporate wellness programs, "well" days instead of sick days and an emphasis on the recreation and leisure benefits of employees. More subtle changes are increasingly infusing the workplace with a play perspective. Workers are being encouraged to think creatively, to become a part of a team, to take pride and a sense of ownership in their work, to be flexible in their working hours and to compete, in a game-like fashion, for incentives.

A playful approach to learning can enhance the nation's education. From its earliest roots, play and scholarship have been intertwined. The word, "schole", denoted both learning and playing in ancient Greek. Through the centuries the concepts diverged in western schools until scholasticism became a polar opposite to playing. Scholasticism eschewed fun in the classroom for it might interfere with the exclusive emphasis on "the life of the mind" and the serious business of mastering and memorizing ideas. The empiricism of the scientific approach that has gained ascendancy in our schools is founded on reductionism: the ability to reduce observed phenomena to measurable proportions and to replicate scientific analysis. The casualty of a system of learning that places a premium on measuring and memorizing is play.

Play in learning involves creating, discovering and even dreaming. Rather than memorizing concepts that may be useful in the marketplace, it entails learning for it's own sake. In the case of physical education it involves identifying and developing the physical attributes of each individual for the purposes of a lifetime of learning, rather than focusing on fostering the skills of the talented few so that they may triumph in athletic competition. Schools rarely prioritize such play qualities as creativity, self-expression and freedom. Rather, schools tend to focus on preparing students for the serious world of work.

The ideology of industrialization and technology permeates the classroom. Students are often produced, defined and refined through a conveyer belt education system, which emphasizes conformity, uniformity and evaluation rather than self-expression, self-realization and self-actualization. Because of its shortcomings, physical education is under siege in financially strapped school systems. The threat of extinction is forcing programs to reassess their style and substance. In recent decades, programs premised on play have become more apparent in schools.

At the elementary level, movement education, with its emphasis on self-discovery, has found a niche. Children are encouraged, but not coerced, to experiment with such dimensions as time, weight, space and flow through exploratory movement. The process is cooperative rather than competitive and above all it should be fun. Similarly at the secondary levels, such innovative and creative play settings as ropes courses, "New Games" and outdoor adventure education supplement more traditional sports and games skills in some progressive physical education curricula. These programs utilize the beauty, complexity and potential danger of experiencing the natural world "hands on" and at close range to reinforce the values of cooperation, self-sufficiency, "hard play" and aesthetic appreciation. A growing recognition that traditional approaches to enhancing health and fitness in physical education are meeting with mixed results is breeding innovative initiatives. A fundamental problem is that physical education tends to "preach to the choir".

Programs premised on athletic skill attract talented athletes, but repel the physically challenged who are in many cases the population most in need of physical challenge. The competitive comparative nature of sport is alienating to such individuals because they are perpetually being relegated to the status of second class citizens on the basis of the quality of their physical performance. To reach this disenchanted group of students, innovative physical education is emphasizing play, enjoyment through movement, creativity, problem-solving, choice and a sense of ownership in the process of becoming physically educated.

Even the aspect of schooling to which conventional wisdom would ascribe responsibility for preparation for play is permeated by these qualities of the work world. Sport, a supposed bastion of play, has become so regimented and product-oriented that the work ethic often predominates over the play ethic. Children will tend to gravitate toward playfulness in sport until the adult world looms over their horizon. Fearing that playfulness might interfere with victory, coaches can often be overheard admonishing their young athletes not to "mess around" and to take playing seriously. For many such coaches winning is a very serious business. Their credibility and even their jobs might depend upon their success. No wonder then that compliance is emphasized over creativity and that playing sport for fun often becomes secondary to working at winning.

Review

The discussion and exercises in this chapter have been designed to enhance your understanding, appreciation and experiencing of play. In the first section we analyzed the qualities of the phenomenon in order to build a definition of the play process. Even as we recognized that play will inevitably change through your life span, we recognized that there are certain immutable unchanging aspects to play. The next section could have been subtitled, "So, what's in it for you?" The point of departure for this discussion was Plato's statement that life must be lived as play. The ensuing section encouraged you to think about what living life as play might entail and to consider the alternative. The final segment expanded this analysis to encompass the society of which you are a member by considering the contribution of play to our culture. Throughout the discussion was interspersed an open invitation to you to experience the power of play in your own life.

Chapter 5

APPRECIATING MOVEMENT

Preview

The goal of this chapter is to develop your appreciation of human movement, by:

- examining and experiencing beauty in action,

- encountering aesthetic analysis,

- constructing a personal language of appreciation from an aesthetic alphabet,

- engaging in an ongoing process of seeking and recognizing quality, beauty and joy in and through your physical activity.

The Art and Science of Movement

Kinesiology is the art and science of human movement. The art and the science can coexist amicably in the study of human movement. Good scientists are artists. They think creatively to design innovative research protocols, to analyze their data and to reach valid conclusions. They meticulously attend to their projects as things of beauty, refining their craft in the pursuit of knowledge. Yet, despite this affinity and the growth of the popularity of this approach, the scientific method is not always the friend of the arts in kinesiology. The recent growth of interest in exercise and nutrition, health and healing and performance enhancement has tilted our field of study toward the scientific end of the spectrum. Sub-disciplines such as exercise physiology, biomechanics and motor control "rule the roost". Studies based in the humanities, such as sport literature, sport history and even philosophy are peripheral. The experiencing of movement through physical activity and dance is often marginalized in kinesiology programs that are based on the scientific method. Paradoxically, many of the students who populate this growing field gravitate towards human movement studies because of their own rewarding biographical experiences.

Exercise 5-1: The beauty in the movement of your youth

Does this statement ring true for you? Look back at your life history and recollect movement experiences that have profoundly influenced your study and career choices. Perhaps you remember family times that revolved around outdoor activities or dramatic exploits in Little League or overcoming the traumatic effects of injury.

Discussion: In every case, it was the profound effect of the experience that created an indelible imprint. Most of these childhood treasures transcend science. They cannot be measured, they are beyond statistical analysis, but the experiences you have remembered are an important part of your development. If we are to capture the essence of the meaning of movement in our field, we cannot allow the experiencing of our physical being to be squeezed out of kinesiology. These experiences include parameters that are amenable to scientific analysis, such as cellular and hormonal responses, kinematically measurable patterns of movement and mood states that are accessible through psychological profiling. For a full appreciation of the movement experience art and science must coexist. The effects of the beauty of the moment and the joy of rewarded effort defy science but we can grapple with them through philosophy. The realm of philosophy that can help us to understand the beauty in our movement is aesthetics. Recent aesthetic investigation has been focused on the processes of producing, experiencing and evaluating art and on those aspects of nature and human performance considered to be outside of the realm of art that nevertheless evoke an aesthetic response. We will now proceed to consider sport as art and movement as an aesthetic process.

Sport As Art

If life is a canvas on which we create our own masterpiece, we can all consider ourselves to be artists. You may retort that this can only be true when I am involved in creative activities. Perhaps I may be considered an artist if I compose or perform music, but surely not when I am washing the dishes! The portrayal of Mrs. Doubtfire by Robin Williams suggested that even the most menial tasks can be imbued with artistry, but few would argue that vacuum-cleaning can be considered an art-form. A debate has been raging in the past decades about whether sport can be art.

That sport and art have enjoyed a close relationship through the ages is not a point of contention. The athlete in action has been a popular choice of sculptors and artists since the ancient Greek civilization produced a wealth of artistic artifacts that displayed the Olympic athletes in all their glory. From creations in classical art forms to depictions in popular culture, such as movies, sport has been represented as an object of beauty. However, sport as the subject matter of art is not the same as sport as art. The topic of debate is, can sport, in and of itself, be considered an art form to the extent that it meets the criteria applied to such art forms as sculpting, painting and dance?

Rather than observing this debate from afar as armchair philosophers, it's time to roll up your sleeves and get involved (remember, the underlying theme of this book's approach is that you can only construct a philosophy of life by being actively engaged in the process!).

Exercise 5-2: Is sport art?

art = passion

Debate that sport is an art form. (Notice the congruence with the scientific method here in that the debate is stated as a hypothesis so that it may be disproved or verified through the evidence presented).

This exercise should help you to think through an issue as you consider the topic and construct arguments for and against the motion. As you do so, you will recognize that not only are there two sides to every argument, but that in many cases, there is not a clear-cut verdict. If you have been weaned on the certainty of empiricism, it can be unsettling to enter an academic arena,

- where asking the question can be more important than finding an answer,

- where finding an answer can depend upon the skill you develop in framing the solution and

- where answers that you reach are more likely to be relative shades of gray than absolute black and white.

That is the nature of philosophic analysis, and, as I'm sure you will be quick to point out, that it is also the nature of life. How often are you confronted with major decisions that are simple and clear-cut in your daily existence? Hopefully, involving yourself in the following philosophic process here and now will pay dividends when you are faced with momentous decisions in your future:

Step 1: Look back in the introductory chapter at the discussion of the philosophic decision making process, which entails reacting, self-distancing, identifying, analyzing and synthesizing. The first stages in this case may not be too problematic. This debate, while interesting, may not stir the fires of controversy in the same way as many of the ethical issues we will confront in the next chapter. So, although your reaction to this issue may not be strong, you should have little problem in detaching yourself emotionally from the question, which has already been identified for you.

Step 2: Analyze the motion carefully. A good place to start is with the words, "sport" and "art". The way you interpret these concepts will determine the outcome of the debate. It is tempting to assume that these commonly used words have readily agreed upon meanings. Yet, if you were to ask your friends to freely associate an activity with the concept sport, responses would probably range from football to frisbee. Some would think of sports that have obvious aesthetic appeal, such as gymnastics, diving and synchronized swimming, while others would name auto-racing, boxing and chess, which at first glance seem less artistically appealing. Similarly, questions can be raised about the nature of art. Is art the process or the product, the act of creation or the picture on the canvas? Does an artifact have to be produced with a definite expressive intent in the mind of the creator? Does it necessarily have to express life issues beyond the artistic medium itself?

This question of expressive intent is pivotal to your position. For sport to qualify as an art form it must meet the basic criteria of art. The purpose of the athlete as artist must be synonymous with that of the actor in any other artistic medium. Furthermore, the product of the athlete's endeavors must be a work of art. Given these parameters to your argument, how might you present pro and con?

Step 3: Try it out. Develop arguments for and against the motion. For example:

Pro: that sport is art. The purpose of the Olympic figure skater is to create a thing of beauty. The appearance and presentation of the performer are married with the grace and precision of movement to measure up to an aesthetic ideal. The finished product, the sights and sounds of the highly gifted athlete performing with consummate skill are indeed a work of art. While it is true that athletes may seek fame and fortune through their craft, isn't it also true that artists have to earn a living? Don't artists paint for profit, poets receive remuneration for their work, dancers compete to be accepted into juried shows? In both sport and art the process of expression through a chosen medium creates a product pleasing to the spectator. Each individual develops a unique style of execution and adapts imaginatively to the possibilities of their craft with new techniques and innovative uses of equipment. The athlete is an artist performing in the art form of sport.

Con: that sport is not an art form. The purpose of the athlete is not to create a work of art, but to win. The means to winning is not creativity and expressiveness, but efficiency and functionality. The aesthetic element is incidental in even the artistic tributary of sports and superfluous in the mainstream. In art, the means are the end, whereas in sport the end justifies the means. Sport is about the bottom line, crass commercialism and being number one, not the production of art. Sport is primarily physical, art mental; sport is frequently coach-dominated, art is individualistic; sport can't express concepts of life-issues, art can illuminate the human condition. Although there may be occasional moments of beauty in sport, these are incidental to the action and are only applauded when they lead to victory. Because the motives and methods of athletes and artists are fundamentally different, sport is not an art form.

Step 4: Synthesize your position. Now you get to weigh the balance of the arguments you have been able to martial on each side of the issue. In many ways this philosophic process of synthesis is like the legal process that takes place in the courtroom. You act as judge and jury as you decide which is the stronger argument. Like a hung jury, it may be that you cannot reach a verdict because you cannot differentiate clearly between the two positions, or because the two positions seem to be equally persuasive. Before you abstain, be certain that the reason is not intellectual laziness. Scrutinize the evidence presented more carefully, seek new information from other sources or synthesize your own alternative position, but don't sit on the fence. Life is full of tricky decisions, use this debating process as a form of preparation and practice for the art of decision making.

Sport As Aesthetic

The aesthetic domain extends beyond the realm of art. Aspects of nature and human production can often evoke an aesthetic response during contemplation of their forms or sensory qualities. What you find to be beautiful is idiosyncratic, a unique response that only you can experience to a particular stimulus. The fashion precepts of the age and culture in which you reside will inevitably influence your taste in beauty, but your individual predilections will ultimately determine what you find to be beautiful. Typically, beauty, as in art, is associated with the stationary images of the portrait, the poem or the sculpture. However, given that sport is a dynamic endeavor in which we can all see beauty, such static standards of excellence must be expanded to incorporate the beauty of movement and the unfolding drama of the athletic contest.

To elaborate upon this notion further, a primary focus of aesthetic appreciation has always been the human body. Standards of beauty have changed through the ages (for example, the pendulum of social approval of the female torso has swung between the fecund belly featured in Renaissance art and the pinched abdomen, made popular by such models as Twiggy in the 1960s). Furthermore, the epitome of attractiveness in one culture may not approximate the standards in a distant land. Yet, artists, poets and the person on the street all find beauty in the human form. They may be attracted by the animal magnetism, the apparent virility, the marvelous intricacy of the human anatomy or any number of other factors. Yet, it is the dimension of the body in a state of motion that sport so uniquely provides for aesthetic approval. Sport is a venue for the body to be on display at it's finest. Perhaps you are amazed at the dexterity and adroitness of the sublime execution of a complex skill, or perhaps it is the agonistic struggle in the heat of the contest, or the triumph of the individual over adversity that triggers your aesthetic response.

Another vital component is context. The setting in which sport takes place will influence your aesthetic response. The beauty of nature and the atmosphere in the stadium are examples of context that affect determination of beauty. Running along the shoreline at sunset . . . skiing a powder bowl among the peaks on a brilliant spring day . . . enjoying a championship playoff game from a front row seat . . . these are examples of activities enhanced by their environment. The relationship of individuals with nature, of athletes with their arenas of activity, has been a source of considerable artistic inspiration in itself. From the musings of such poets as William Wordsworth to the paintings of George Bellows and the sculptures of R. Tait McKenzie, the influence of the environment upon the performer is a recurring theme. For example, Wordsworth's poems suggest Nature's nurturing power and focus the attention of the reader upon the senses in aesthetic appreciation. He refers to the sights and sounds of the mountains, forests and waterfalls that colored his experiences as a boy growing up in the Lake District. Sensory input is a fundamental factor in the determination of beauty.

Experiencing the Aesthetic

While discussing the aesthetic may help to focus our attention on the moving body, the context of our actions and the sensory satisfaction that a particular moment might bring, the only way to appreciate beauty is by experiencing it your self.

Exercise 5-3: Moving with beauty in mind

Select one activity that you enjoy and as you engage in it, pay particular attention to your body, your feelings and your senses. Jot down notes immediately afterwards to help clarify your aesthetic response.

Specimen Response: To help you in this exercise, here is one such description from Keith, an undergraduate student at the College of William and Mary:

"While running I am at complete peace. Running clears my mind and allows me to experience the aesthetics of motion. The motion, while rather simple, is very graceful. The complete body is at ease with every stride. All of the body parts are working as one, without any thought. Running is graceful and fluid. I feel as if I am a drop of rain moving freely as it falls from a cloud. With every breath I feel more at ease. My nose is breathing the sweet autumn air that is forced against my face. The air, with it's slight chill, is channeled down into my lungs. I feel my lungs expanding. They feel full. Without any hesitation the air is gone and I am looking forward to the next. My body does not ache. I am entranced by the sound of the wind passing by my ears, it seems to be whispering something to me. And the sights, I see so much more and I experience so much more when interacting with the environment one on one. I see trees changing colors. I smell leaves burning and hear water splashing on a rocky riverbed. Not only am I experiencing the body in motion. I am enjoying how motion can be performed. I am not running for the external beauty. I am running for the feelings, the emotions, the grace, the beauty that a movement can bring me while I am performing an activity."

Discussion: Keith vividly describes his sensations and his feelings as he performs an activity. As you participate in the activity of your choice, try to focus deeply on your own inner functioning. Start with your breathing pattern. Concentrate on the rhythms of your body. Observe not only your own movements, but also your surroundings. See the colors, smell the air, feel the breeze. Be as aware as you can of what causes your activity to be a rewarding experience.

You can appreciate beauty by looking both inward and outward. Beauty is not only in the performing, but also in the beholding.

Exercise 5-4: Watching movement with beauty in mind

Select an activity that you like to watch and record the sources of your aesthetic appreciation as the spectacle unfolds.

Specimen Response: An example, in which Rebecca observed college basketball players, may help you in this analysis:

"In examining the team as a whole, I noticed several characteristics which I found to be aesthetically pleasing. I watched the flow of the players move across the floor with rapid movements as the ball continuously changed possession. The players moved as if they were swarms of bees moving so fast that they seemed to fly. The constant momentum of their movements created a floating appearance only to be interrupted by the sound of a whistle. Just as the undulating mass of players started to become hypnotic a turnover, foul or buzzer would grab my attention and draw me back into the game. The momentum changed as the score became closer building a tension that left me pleasantly waiting for the unexpected or spontaneous burst of energy within the continuous rhythm of the game. When I looked more specifically at the movements of the team as a whole, strategies became apparent. The teams would complete complicated patterns of passes and movements in order to move around the opposing team and to take the open shot. These patterns created a visual design on the court as the colored jerseys swirled around each other, almost as if in a kaleidoscope."

Discussion: In this account of the basketball team, Rebecca found beauty in a team event far removed from the grace and refinement of such artistic sports as gymnastics and diving. Born in the sweaty, all-male setting of a Springfield gym, basketball has grown up in the poverty and violence of the inner city. At first glance, this "in your face", trash-talking activity may not seem to be a viable candidate for aesthetic analysis. Yet, for Rebecca, a well-conceived play, a skilfully executed strategy and the sight of five superb athletes acting in unison, striving and moving together to reach the same goal, were things of beauty.

Aesthetics is not only the domain of the dainty. Many spectators find joy in the rugged features of the game: the sheer power, the attempt to dominate, the physical confrontation. For others, the intellectual dimensions of both players and coaches planning and implementing strategies to nullify the advantages of the opposing forces, while maximizing their own perceived strengths is the essence of beauty in the game. For most observers, the physical prowess of an outstanding player, such as Michael Jordan who seems to perform with such consummate form, is aesthetically pleasing.

Exercise 5-5: Aesthetic analysis

Aesthetically analyze a team sport, trying to describe the beauty in both the group effort and the exploits of the individual players.

Specimen Response: "The individual players fascinated me with their physical strength and accomplishments. I noticed the perfectly arched flight of the player slam-dunking the ball, his smooth take-off and his apparent weightlessness. Although this occurred many times throughout the game, no two players were the same and each dunk left me in awe. Besides appreciating this apparent effortlessness, I could also appreciate the strength and amazing skill required to accomplish the task. The players struggled against gravity, and won. They also appeared to move with grace as they completed perfect jump shots from the three point line. The connectedness of the stop, the preparation, the aim and, finally, the shot created a continuous sequence of perfectly timed movement."(Rebecca)

Expressing The Aesthetic

Our language is limited. How often do you find that you have experienced something very special, but when you try to share that moment with someone else, words fail you? It is, by definition, impossible to express the ineffable. The magic of the aesthetic experience often seems ineffable: difficult to understand and virtually impossible to express. However, unless we decide to live a life of solitude, to experience but not to share through our limited powers of communication, we had better keep on working on our words and our images. You will notice that, in order to convey the meaning of the aesthetic moment more clearly, both Keith and Rebecca resorted to the descriptive devices of imagery. Analogies, metaphors and similes are among the literary techniques that can be used to clarify and enhance mutual understanding. For example, Keith equates his running experience with a drop of rain falling from a cloud and Rebecca describes the tenacious group cohesion of the basketball team "as a swarm of bees moving so fast they seemed to fly". Comparisons will help to convey meaning, but there is no substitute for a full and comprehensive vocabulary. This Aesthetic Alphabet might help:

	Aesthetic Alphabet			
A	action	artistry		
B	balance			
C	clothing	color	context	control
D	danger	disguise	dynamic	
E	efficient	effort	emotion	execute	expertise
F	flow	fluidity	force	form
G	grace			
H	harmony			

I	ideal	illusion					
J	joy						
K	kinesic						
L	lovely						
M	might						
N	natural						
O	original						
P	poise	power					
Q	quality						
R	rhythm	risk					
S	shape	skill	speed	strategy	strength	style	slickness
T	tactics	tempo	tension	timing			
U	unity						
V	victory	virtue					
W	winning						
X	Xellence (sorry!)						
Y	youthful						
Z	zeal	zest					

The Aesthetic Alphabet is only a beginning. You are aware of words that can help you to define a moment of beauty but which don't appear on this list. Use them in conjunction with this alphabet to augment your vocabulary and enrich your aesthetic expression.

Exercise 5-6: Expressing the aesthetic

Try describing a beautiful movement experience, selecting qualitative words carefully from the alphabetical list and from your own vocabulary. Allow your imagination to range through images that will help you to bring your experience to life for the listener.

Discussion: In a very real way you are "playing" with words as you creatively reconstruct a beautiful moment in meaningful language. You are authoring poetry in motion. This description is poetic in that, just as the movement experience itself defies and transcends the medium of words, so the words you select should transcend the mundane and prosaic. Phrases such as, "it was neat" (nice, cool, awesome, etc.) which might be adequate in normal conversation, don't come close to capturing the magic of an aesthetically pleasing experience. Even the most poetic language rich with imagery and carefully selected descriptors will fail to do the experience justice. Words, as a form of symbolic communication are simply not fully adaptable to the language of sport. The marriage between artistry in action and the articulation of action through words is strained.

The reconciliation of movement and it's expression has been a project of pioneers in the human movement field this century. Rudolph Laban developed a movement notation system that has informed the evolution of modern dance and branches of pedagogical theory. Eleanor Metheny proposed a general theory of the meaning of human movement consisting of kinestructs, kinescepts and kinesymbols, which she named kinesthesia. The field of Somatic Studies has continued the process of appreciating and expressing the lived-body experience with the prompting of such leaders as Tom Hanna and Sy Kleinman.

Follow in their footsteps as you seek new and better ways of experiencing the joy and beauty of your movement experiences and as you develop more refined ways of understanding their significance in your own life and of giving them meaning through dialogue.

Evaluating The Aesthetic

Knowing that a movement is beautiful doesn't mean that we understand why it is. Such knowledge entails aesthetic sensitivity rather than aesthetic judgement. Given that "beauty is in the eye of the beholder", it may well be that universal criteria of aesthetic judgement are an unreasonable expectation. Individual preferences may preclude any commonality in the perception of beauty. Indeed, neither humanistic-philosophic nor scientific-empirical modes of enquiry have been able to discover unequivocal, universal standards for measuring beauty in movement.

On the other hand, "form sports", such as gymnastics, diving and figure skating, which have become very popular in recent years, are premised upon a universally accepted aesthetic ideal. Successful performance entails conforming as closely as possible to a pre-conceived, shared epitome of perfection. It is quite possible that one of the reasons for the fascination of the viewing public is that they share this official version of what is deemed to be beautiful. They like to be armchair judges using the same criteria as the Olympic officials, for example, to reach their own conclusions about the beauty of a particular performance. Is it possible, then, that there exist common, shared criteria of beauty in motion?

Exercise 5-7: Evaluating the aesthetic

Try an aesthetic experiment at this point to test out the hypothesis that we all share common perceptions of what constitutes beauty in sport. Make a list of the ingredients of sporting performance that you consider beautiful. Such a list might include, but not be limited to, the following:

1. Technical excellence in execution.

2. Expression of deeply felt emotion.

3. Struggle against adversity.

4. Perceptible pleasure - the joy of effort.

5. Functional fluidity - grace, economy and efficiency

6. Appropriate appearance - the body beautiful.

7. Stimulating sights and sounds

8. Striking setting - the wonders of Nature.

9. Flow - an altered state of peak performance.

10. Group cohesion - team unity and support.

Take the list of criteria that you develop through your own experiences and put "meat on their bones" by fleshing them out with your own actual, lived aesthetic moments. To test the hypothesis of universally accepted standards of beauty, share your own criteria with others. The level of congruence in perceptions of what constitutes beauty in sport will prove or disprove your hypothesis. What are your conclusions?

Review

Beauty in sport is often experienced, but seldom studied. It is a primary reason for the popularity of sport. It is a venue in which people can experience movement in pleasing ways; feelings of control and competence and even beauty in their own motion and the vicarious appreciation of the agony and ecstacy of others performing. Yet, because beauty defies empirical description, it tends to be absent from the art and science of movement except as a form of performing art, such as in the case of Dance. This is a sad state of affairs, for the aesthetic moment is one of special significance. We are excited by skilled sports performance in which such qualities as speed, strength and strategy are employed to explore human limitations. We enjoy participating for the personal experience of mastery and the vision of beauty we see in our own motion. The premise of this chapter has been that we should not shy away from the richness of the aesthetic experience in, and through, sport. In fact we should take every opportunity to seek it out and we should appreciate it as fully as we can. In the process, it is incumbent upon us, as educated human beings, to understand and discuss the indefinable. Rather than ignoring the ineffable, we should accept the challenge of exploring uncharted territories of human experience. Although words cannot fully reconstruct our movement reality, we can strive to improve our expression and our evaluation of the aesthetic moment.

Part IV

CHOOSING THE RIGHT PATH

Chapter 6

MAKING MORAL CHOICES

Preview

This chapter will help you to explore and understand the ethics behind your own decision-making and it will provide you with a framework for evaluating the moral choices of others. The emphasis on applied ethics will empower you to think and act for yourself. It will help you to recognize when and where an ethical choice must be made, it will provide you with ethical "tools" to reach the best decision and it will help you to evaluate the action that should be taken in the context of that decision.

Specifically in this chapter you will find

- a discussion of the growing need for ethics in the health and human movement fields,

- a familiar theoretical framework that has been adopted for philosophical thinking throughout this book and that is now adapted to provide you with a grounding for comprehensive ethical decisions,

- exercises that will help you to establish ethical principles to follow as you put theory into practice.

The Growing Need for Ethics

Health and human movement are fertile fields indeed for applied ethics. Changes in health care have produced an array of perplexing moral dilemmas. The need for biomedical ethics has grown dramatically as our technical capabilities have expanded. Advances in science and technology have enabled health care professionals to affect the circumstances of life and death and have forced the general public to confront a whole new array of technical dilemmas. Ranging from birth (e.g. cloning, genetic intervention and abortion) to death (e.g. euthanasia, physician-assisted suicide and organ transplantation), health care is entering territory where technical ability is only part of the answer. Because we can do it is not a good enough rationale. More important is whether we <u>should</u> do it. This is the province of ethics.

Health related issues extend beyond the medical realm to encompass personal health, community health and environmental health. Maintaining your personal health can involve moral as well as technical or procedural issues. For example, weight loss can be an issue fraught with moral questions. The epidemic of eating disorders (such as bulimia) is often living proof of "wrong" answers. Personal health habits are premised upon personal values. Tobacco, alcohol and recreational drug choices reflect more than your taste, they are a testament to your moral code. The way you live reflects your value-system. Your personal health habits are your applied ethics. Similarly, your attitudes and actions towards your community are based on your ethical stance. The quality of your interactions with individuals and institutions that you encounter are premised upon your philosophy of life. Such philosophic foundations as the purpose and meaning of life and your interpretation of human nature are going to influence the way you relate to others. Moral choice, or your determination of the right way to relate to others, will decide whether your relationships are manipulative and exploitative or mutually affirming and supportive.

Community health is premised on service. Whether you choose to be involved in the giving and helping relationships that are the foundation of service will depend upon whether you decide it is right to do so. Similarly, environmental health is correlated with moral choice. Whether to pollute or clean up, to litter or pick up, to nurture or kill non-human denizens of the environment are questions you encounter daily that reflect your moral code. Your attitudes towards hunting and animal research, protecting wild habitats from development or defending an endangered species are grounded in your philosophy. How you decide to use or abuse your environment is a matter of moral choice.

Exercise 6-1: Health and Morality: Identifying Issues

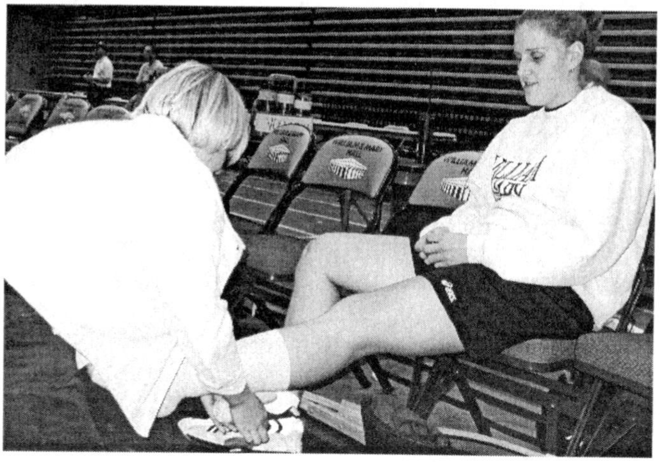

HEALTH

		Medical	~~Personal~~	Community	Environmental
D	Ever (Other)	Mom - diabetes		Hab. for Hum.	~~Hybrid~~ Animal testing
e	Ever (Self)	Charles → Knee		~~Roads to OBX~~ ~~dumping oil~~	
c	Recent (Other)	Spinal taps	drugs	cloning	Hybrid
i					
s	Recent (Self)			Pools in OBX	dumping oil
i					
o	Current (Other)		Friend w/ anti-depressant	off-campus living	oil crisis
n	Current (Self)	Chuck - following Dr.	Way to run a cappella group		living w/ friends who don't recycle

In the chart above put a couple of words in each matrix to signify a particular ethical decision. Each of the areas of health from the preceding section are listed in the horizontal axis (medical, personal, community and environmental health). The vertical axis represents the continuum of time ranging from the most significant ethical decision **ever** that you can remember, through moral choices in **recent** memory (let's say the past couple of years) to ethical decisions that are **current**. Within each time frame identify one situation that you know about but in which you have no stake (**other**) and one ethical decision in which you are the stakeholder who must decide the right course of action (**self**).

Movement morality is like health ethics in that it is a highly visible, increasingly vital feature of your philosophy. Because your movement is so obvious, you display your ethics in a tangible and telling way. Because technology is increasing our options and the market place is increasing the rewards of success, ethical decision-making is becoming increasingly essential to our performance. Whether you are a player, an administrator, a volunteer, a coach, a spectator, a parent or a teacher you will encounter dilemmas that require you to make moral choices. Issues that are revolutionizing the most popular form of movement, sport, are both a matter of personal choice and of public policy.

As a participant in a sporting event, you have to make choices about how you will play. Some of these choices are of a technical skill-related nature (e.g. how to grip the racket) and some are more tactical and strategic (e.g. whether to bunt or swing, or whether to drive to the basket or to step back and shoot the three-pointer). But the decisions you make that will most profoundly affect the quantity and the outcome of the game are ethical in nature. You must make decisions about rules and regulations, such as whether to observe the letter or the spirit of the laws of the game, whether to play by the rules or by the rules as interpreted by an official, or even whether to play by the rules at all. You must make ethical decisions about strategy, such as whether to attempt to deceive your opponent by engaging in strategic deception (pretending to make one move with the intention of doing something different) or definitional deception (breaking the rules while pretending to observe them). Most importantly, you must make moral choices about how you will treat your fellow participants (teammates and opponents) by answering in theory and in action such questions as,

- Will you observe the basic tenets of sportsmanship or of "one-upmanship"?

- Are your actions going to be governed by a respect and concern for others or will you approach fellow participants as obstacles for you to manipulate in your single minded pursuit of the goal of winning, without any regard for their health or well-being?

- Will you cheat, foul, intimidate and hurt your opponents to reach that goal? Answers to these questions are complicated by the circumstances and are rarely clear-cut (Could you say categorically that you would never break a rule or that you would always cheat to win?). Yet most of us would define some limits that are based upon moral principles (perhaps you would agree that you would never act in such a way that you would intentionally harm another player). The way that you participate in competitive physical activity is prescribed and proscribed by your ethical decisions.

Similarly, as a leader, guide or mentor (teacher, coach, volunteer or parent), your involvement in the game is fraught with ethical decisions. What will you teach your students of sport beyond skills and strategy? Do you teach them to observe the rule or to get away with what they can, (to make their own line calls or to break the rules without getting caught)? In many cases there is no easy answer. For example, you

will almost certainly be involved in a lopsided contest at some time, which will involve you in the ethical dilemma of whether to instruct your players to run up the
score. How will you react? Will you tell your players to take it easy on the opponents, juggle your line up, change the way you play to decrease the chance of scoring, or do you carry on playing as usual with the expectation of scoring as highly as
possible? Again, your decision will be determined by your moral principles, but the
interpretation of these principles is problematic. Perhaps you decide to act in such a
way that you show respect to your opponents. If so, is it respectful to "soften the
blow" or could that course of action be interpreted as "adding insult to injury" by
showing not only that your team is superior, but that it can beat the weaker team
without really trying! Sport is ethics in action, a boiling cauldron of moral choices
that frequently bubble up in the heat of the moment. It is a setting that increasingly
requires reflective moral judgement as the professional ethic of big-time sports per-
colates down through the ranks of youth and amateur sports.

Sport is a global economic force with universal political and profit power. As
sport becomes a commodity, we become its producers and consumers. As producers
and consumers we come together to exchange the goods and services of the sports
industry. This process of commodification of sport involves us all in the policies and
practices of professionalization that affects sport at every level. The power of profit
has elevated sport into the top tier of entertainment industries in the latter part of
the twentieth century. It has become one of the most ubiquitous fixtures of the mass
media. Sport is watched on a daily basis by a large proportion of the viewing public.
Major events such as the Olympic Games, World Cup Soccer and the Superbowl are
the most watched spectacles on television. Sports heroes are household names, sports
are a frequent topic of conversation, sports have become a universal language. Such
popularity has brought fame and fortune to many associated with the sports business. This includes primary producers, such as players, coaches, administrators,
mass media and sports marketers. It also includes secondary producers such as the
sport clothing, shoe and retail industry, restaurant, hotel and travel providers, and
the gaming enterprises that profit from gambling on the outcome of sporting events.
All of these groups have considerable interest in the success of sporting ventures. It
is no wonder, then, that the growth in professionalism has been infused with an
emphasis on winning, on commercial viability and upon the capitalistic ethic. The
emphasis upon "professional conduct," which implied moral rectitude, has been supplanted by the era of "the professional foul" – a cynical, win-at-all-costs strategy.
The ethic of capitalism, based upon the profit motive, is permeating sport at all
levels. Young people see their sport heroes as role models. They inevitably recognize the relationship between winning and wealth, the mercenary attitude of the
top professional athletic and agent bargaining to become millionaires, the urgency
of getting an edge over competitors by any means. The impact of commodification
upon the nature of sport is profound. As the mass media fans the flames of the
professionalization of sport, ethics is serving as a firewall between the commodified
sport industry and the general public. Although we may hear about performance
enhancing drug use by elite athletes or cynical professional fouls, intimidation and

violence in the pursuit of victory, it is individual ethics that will ultimately determine our course of action. As producers and consumers of sport, we are not sponges, soaking up all that we see later to replicate these behaviors, but we are discerning, discriminating agents, able to determine for ourselves what we should do in a given sports setting and why we should act that way.

Exercise 6-2: Movement and Morality: Identifying Issues

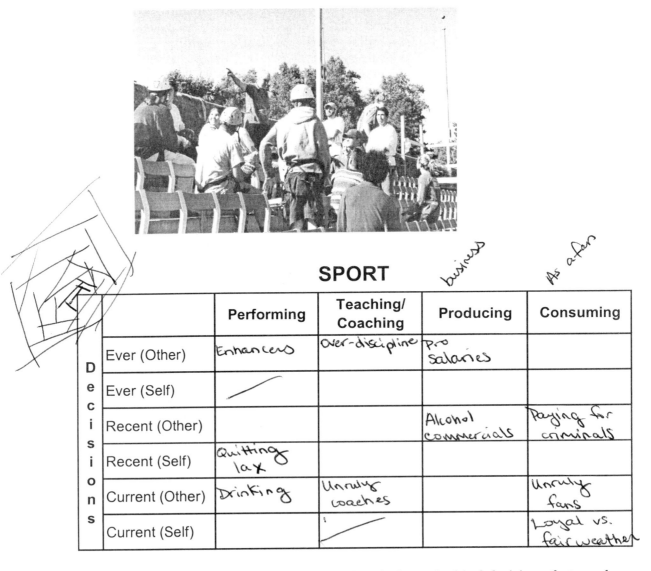

SPORT

		Performing	Teaching/ Coaching	Producing *business*	Consuming *As a fan*
D	Ever (Other)	Enhancers	Over-discipline	Pro salaries	
e	Ever (Self)	/			
c					
i	Recent (Other)			Alcohol commercials	Paying for criminals
s					
i	Recent (Self)	Quitting lax			
o	Current (Other)	Drinking	Unruly coaches		Unruly fans
n					
s	Current (Self)		/		Loyal vs. fair weather

In the chart above, write brief descriptions of ethical decisions that you have made (self) or witnessed (other) in each category. This exercise is designed to involve you in the process of applied ethics by recognizing ethical dilemmas that are part of your sport history.

How to Make Ethical Decisions

Reacting. Recognizing and reacting to ethical issues in your daily existence is the starting point in the process of making ethical decisions. This first step in making moral choices is often a tough step to take, particularly for those who are afflicted by a moral blind spot. They do not see the ethics in a situation for a variety of reasons. They may be morally immature, not yet adept at reasoning in a philosophic way. For example, they may accept the advantages of technology as being reason enough to act without considering the question of whether life sustaining or performance-enhancing innovations <u>should</u> always be used. Alternatively, they may consciously sidestep the moral issue. Perhaps they understand their action to be strategic rather than ethical, such as in the case of the intentional foul. Or, perhaps they absolve themselves of the personal responsibility for making the ethical decision by deferring it to some higher authority that has stated an official position on how to act in such a situation. The higher authority may be a person in a position of power (e.g. coach, doctor, teacher) or a professional organization (e.g. NCAA, AMA) or a binding ideology (e.g. Hippocratic Oath, laws of the land, religious dogma). But perhaps, the greatest reason of all for not recognizing and reacting to an ethical issue is the moral callusing of our culture. Behavior that seemed unethical a generation ago may be commonplace today. For example, in reaching the final stages of medicine (death) or sport (winning) standards have changed. Sanctity of life has been replaced by quality of life as the primary determinant of whether a patient should be allowed to die. Technological changes coupled with advancements in medical care, particularly ventilators and ICUs, have immersed the medical community and the general public in ethical debates about the definition of death, the meaning of personhood and the responsibilities of the care-giver. Similarly the advances in performance technology, in equipment design and, most importantly, in the payoff for success have involved the sports community and the general public in debates over the validity of the behavior, the methods and the bottom line of the new generation of multi-millionaire athletes. For some, these debates are urgent, heated and meaningful, but to many they are distant and immaterial. This latter group may have become morally callused by the widespread magnitude of practices that are generally accepted. They may go beyond the lackadaisical response that, "there's nothing I can do about it" to the position of accepting similar behavior in their own lifestyle, because "every one is doing it."

The first stage of the ethical decision making process is to overcome the problems of moral inertia and cultural callusing, to acknowledge that there is a dilemma and that it is ethically laden. Without such reflective recognition, the decision-maker will proceed to take a course of action that is premised upon an unconscious ethical bias. This first stage of reacting entails developing ethical vision and an appetite for making moral choices. Ethical decision making is a proactive process that may involve an element of discomfort. Whereas the immature philosopher may take the path of least resistance, recognizing and reacting to an ethical dilemma may entail taking a stand, going against the flow of popular opinion.

Self-Distancing. Ethical analysis is a reflective process, but ethical dilemmas are often encountered in the heat of the contest or in the tense and intense setting of the emergency room. Initial reactions to the issue can be intense. Faced with a cheater, you may naturally want to act in the same way or to punish the individual for apparent transgressions. Reactions may be visceral, emotional and even violent. Dealing with a situation where a loved one is in danger, it may be difficult to take a step toward mental detachment to consider the larger picture, but good ethical decision making requires an element of self-distancing. It may often be that your first reaction is not the best reaction. Actions that you would take in the heat of the moment may create more complications than they solve. Although total objectivity is certainly an unreasonable expectation, and is probably philosophically unattainable, an element of detached objectivity will tend to lead to a more reasoned and reasonable response to an ethical stimulus.

Self-distancing means more than detachment. It entails the consideration of self-interest. One response to an ethical dilemma is to ask what is in this situation for me and to act in such a way that personal benefits are maximized. This principle of maximizing personal gain, while it is certainly selfish, may be arrived at through a reflective ethical decision making process. It may also be in conflict with your ethical responsibility to the group involved in a given situation. In such cases of conflict, a process of self-distancing can lead to a demarcation of moral responsibilities to self from those to others. Self-distancing is a prerequisite to choosing a path between personal and public gain.

Identifying. The first two stages of reacting and self-distancing have got you in the ethical ball-park. You have recognized that there is an ethical dilemma and you have positioned yourself to begin the decision-making process in a relatively detached philosophic stance, but you will not be close to reaching your decision until you engage in the process of identifying. Identifying is a focussed form of reacting. Where reacting entails recognizing that there is an ethical dilemma that should be addressed, identifying entails differentiating that root problem from the symptoms. It is an exercise in perspicacity, in which you must not only see the situation clearly, but also pick out the issues that most need addressing. Just as it is poor medical practice to treat the symptoms without effecting total healing, it is a poor ethical response that does not recognize and address the basic issues. Ethical dilemmas are rarely simple or one-dimensional. They generally include a large cast of characters and an array of intentions, sub plots and consequences. Like a skilled detective, you must identify the key players, the most compelling evidence and establish a hierarchy of ethical issues. This hierarchy will provide priorities for your future analysis of the ethical dilemma.

Analysis. Analysis is a process of critical thinking. Ethical analysis involves the generation of alternative courses of action and the evaluation of each of these alternatives. The first form of analysis is a constructive thoughtful creative process of reflective brainstorming. The second form of analysis entails critically analyzing each of the alternatives against pre-established criteria. The rationale is to be ethically comprehensive throughout this process of analysis. To reach good, right and authentic solutions, you will need to draw on ethical theory that establishes how questions of what constitutes a good outcome, a right action and authentic behavior can be resolved. These issues are addressed through teleological, deontological and existential theories of ethical decision making.

Teleological theory focuses upon the consequences of an act in determining good behavior. The basic determinant of the best course of action is the end or result of the act, not the means or process. The good outcome may be subjective and personal, as in the personal pleasure and gratification that is the goal of hedonism, or it may be more objective and generalized to mean the good of a group or society. This latter theory of consequentialism, conceptualized as utilitarianism, is understood to mean that the best course of action is one that will create the greatest good for the greatest number. This may entail taking any course of action that will lead to this result (act utilitarianism) or following rules that are expected to lead to the intended consequence (rule utilitarianism). To evaluate the relative value of several competing courses of action, you can resort to the subjective method of measuring the value of each approach using a form of hedonistic calculus. This entails assessing the ratio of utiles (units of utility) for each alternative to determine which will lead to the greatest good. Although the utilitarian approach to ethical decision making does have the advantage of being oriented toward the future, of being somewhat measurable and of being focussed on the greater good of society, it can also be criticized for shortcomings associated with each of these virtues. The future is hard to predict and even tougher to prepare for. Even best laid plans may fall far short of their intended consequences. Furthermore, this future-orientation is open to the abuse of justifying the means on the basis of the ends, of cheating in order to win, of minor genocide to reach the goal of world peace. Measuring goodness, using utilitarian calculus, is a fine idea, but it is premised upon the notion that goodness can be quantified. Perhaps the most problematic element of utilitarianism is not so much its emphasis upon the outcome for the majority, but the implicit issue that the concerns and welfare of the minority are not important.

Deontological decision making focuses not upon the consequence of the act, but upon the rightness of the act itself. The rightness of the act cannot be measured through utilitarian calculus but is based upon a sense of what is universally right. This sense may be innately derived from an existential feeling of what is the right thing to do. In this case, it is right because it feels authentic and genuine. As an existentialist, you are not acting in accordance with someone else's standards of behavior. You are picking your own way through the dilemma, doing what feels right and acknowledging that ultimately the responsibility for your actions will be yours. Alternatively, the rightness of the action may be based upon some social code of behavior. Such codes take alternative forms, they

- may be theological (perhaps ordained through a holy book),

- may be in the form of a social contract (such as the secular rules designed to promote civilized society),

- may be the product of reasoned intuition (such as the categorical imperative based on duty that Kant proposed as a universal law).

Such deontological perspectives have the advantage of focussing on the manner and intent of our action itself, but they do leave open the question of interpretation. Should such rules be followed blindly? If not, how should we interpret them? This is a particular problem given that these rules, laws and codes are based in tradition which makes them suspect as a prototype for the complexities of the future.

Ultimately, the ethical evaluation of alternative courses of action may hinge upon both teleological and deontological measures. You may select one approach at the expense of the other. For example you might focus on the right outcome without worrying about the morality of the process used to reach a desired end. However, the ideal choice is one in which you select the most right course of action (deontological) with the intent of reaching the best possible outcome (teleological). This right course of action should not only focus on the rules or norms that you choose to govern your behavior (deontological), but also how genuine and authentic this act feels to you (existential).

Exercise 6-3: Analyzing your ethical solution

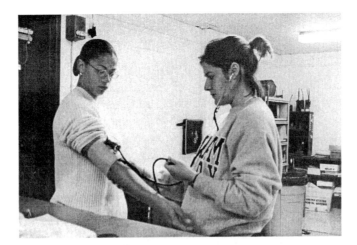

To find the most good, right and authentic solution to an ethical dilemma, ask yourself the following questions about each of the alternatives that you generate through the brainstorming process:

a) Does it accomplish the best end for you (hedonism) and the greatest number (utilitarianism)?

b) Is it consistent with the norms and values of the rules, code or creed that you choose to govern your behavior? To further establish the validity of this course of action, ask (i) would this be free, honest and authentic behavior? (existential), (ii) would you be fulfilling your duty according to these norms and values?

On the "Ethical Decision-Making Analysis" chart assign a maximum score of 25 to each choice on each of the following criteria.

Using the chart, you can make a rational and informed evaluation of the rightness of the process and the goodness of the product of each decision. By quantifying your ethical decision-making you can derive a range of relative merit of each course of action on a scale of 1-100. At the completion of this stage of analysis you should be prepared to move to the all-important final stage of selecting your course of action.

Synthesis. Synthesizing the ideal solution entails choosing and acting upon the most comprehensively good, right and authentic alternative. However, this is not so much an exercise in the highly theoretical realm of metaethics, as it is a real life challenge for you. This is applied ethics, which means that you must select a solution that best fits you and that you will be ready and willing to implement. Consequently, the best decision is not necessarily the one that earned the highest number on the ethical decision making chart. Your decision and your action will be premised upon the unique conditions of your own personality and predicament and upon your commitment to act on your intentions.

ETHICAL DECISION-MAKING ANALYSIS					
		Teleological		Deontological	
		Good Consequence		Right Action	
		Self	Greatest #	Authentic	Duty
Course of Action	1				
	2				
	3				
	4				

Personality considerations include your ethical orientation, the level of your moral development and your demographic profile. Your personality is a complex phenomenon, based in your genetic inheritance and formed through your interactions as you mature. Because we all have different personalities, it is reasonable to assume that we would all respond differently to ethical dilemmas. It would be overly simplistic to suggest that in ethics one size of solution fits all. Although there may be general agreement that certain actions are right or wrong, it is less likely that a consensus could be reached that a particular course of action should be prescribed for all in a given situation. Ethical decision making is ultimately a personal and private process of determining the action that you, alone, should take. Your choice will be a product of your personality. You will have developed an ethical orientation that will color your choices. This may well be an eclectic mix, a combination of teleological deontological and existential predilections. If you have normally responded to a situation with any of the following attitudes:

- that it is important to succeed at all costs,

- or that winning and losing are not as important as how you play the game

- or that it is best to just play in your way,

you will probably tend to like that approach to the ethical dilemma you are facing.

A second important feature of your personality make up is your moral maturity. Your moral behavior is a product of your cognitive complexity. Kohlberg provides a model that helps to explain why stages of cognitive moral development (pre-conventional, conventional and post-conventional) will affect, and even determine, the ethical decision you will make. If you are at the pre-conventional stage, you will tend to act in a hedonistic fashion, your choices will be premised upon personal pleasure, the avoidance of pain and the prospect of profit. At the conventional level you will be more focussed on the effects of your action on significant others and the betterment of society at large. At the post-conventional stage, you will be unselfishly promoting such values as caring and justice as they relate to your profession and your personal and physical environment. Finally, such features of your demographic profile as your age, your level of education, your gender, ethnicity and cultural background are likely to be a factor in your determination of what is right and wrong. The selection of the ideal solution is a process of choosing a course of action that is consistent with such determinants of your personality as your ethical orientation, your cognitive moral development and your demographic profile.

Your ethical stance is also a derivative of your predicament. Your predicament is the situation in which you find yourself as you face a particular ethical dilemma. Significant others, such as family, teammates, fellow workers will tend to mitigate your response. For example, you might choose one course of action, except that you do not want to hurt a loved one, or it is important to you that you please or impress your coach. A second feature of a particular predicament that may influence your ethical decision is its impact. Impact incorporates your perception of how important this issue is to you and how empowered you feel to effect change. If the consequences of your act are likely to have a direct and profound personal impact and if your actions are likely to directly affect the outcome, you will tend to be more focussed in your decision-making. Thirdly, the ideological climate of the setting in which you find yourself will affect your decision-making. In other words, if the norm has been to behave in a particular way ("the way we do things around here"), it can be more problematic to break with tradition. For example, it would take fortitude to be the first member of a tennis, basketball, volleyball or soccer team to start making line calls against yourself that you thought the umpire or referee had missed!

Your personality and predicament will affect your choice. Your intention and commitment will determine whether your choice is transformed into action. If your intention is to carry out an ideal resolution, then presumably you will. However, as the saying goes, "the pathway to hell is paved with good intentions." The point of applied ethics is not to make a decision, but to act on that decision, to initiate change, to right the wrong. This involves having the right intentions and the commitment to stay the course. Acting ethically can be an uncomfortable and demanding endeavor. It can entail treading on people's toes, hurting their feelings and alienating your colleagues. It can lead to personal pain and suffering. In the case of some martyrs, such as Martin Luther King, acting on moral principle has even lead to death. Doing ethics is more than thinking about solutions, it involves acting ethically and having the commitment to bear the consequences.

Exercise 6-4: Synthesizing the Ideal Moral Choice

CONDITIONS

Immediacy: now or far away *setting*

		Ethical Orientation	Moral Development	Demographic Profile	Significant Others	Impact	Ideological Climate
C h o i c e s	1		✓	✓	✓	✓	✓
	2						
	3						

Use the chart above to determine which of the solutions you tested in Exercise 3 best meets the criteria of the ideal moral choice. Consider the conditions that will moderate and modify your choice and list them in the appropriate column. Bear in mind that the ultimate task of your choice will be to follow through and act upon it.

Review and Preview

Sport is ethics in action. Health and medicine are beset with ethical problems. Your movement and your daily interactions are premised on moral choices. Ethics is no longer an option but a personal imperative. You must make ethical choices. So far in this chapter, we have identified some of the ways that ethics are increasingly intruding into your existence and we have suggested ways of confronting ethical issues that will help to make you the master of your own fate. This system of ethical decision-making involves the initial skills of reacting, self-distancing and identifying the issues. At this stage, you are ready to analyze alternatives and ultimately to synthesize the ideal solution.

Now, it is time to delve into the realms of health and human movement. With the help of examples and exercises, we will use our decision-making system to reach judgements about particular issues. We will identify underlying moral principles and begin the process of determining where we stand in relationship to them. Ultimately our goal is to discover and develop our own ethical code. The purpose of this section is to help you to establish your own ethics, to evaluate, test and reevaluate your own ethical decision-making process.

Putting Theory Into Practice

As the old English saying goes, "the proof of the pudding is in the eating." In other words the ingredients of our ethical decision-making system are in place, but they are no more useful then any other theoretical construct until we test them in the real world. This system has a broad application. It is useful in every ethical dilemma, but in this case we will focus it upon issues that commonly arise in the health and human movement-related fields of medicine, sport and education. These issues will be traced back to the basic moral principles that are in question. The examples that we will focus on here are Justice and Equality, Individual Autonomy and Paternalism and The Good Life.

Justice and Equality

Justice has long been a source of ethical debate. Aristotle argued that justice is the whole of virtue and that lack of justice is the whole of vice. He proposed that justice is proportionate in his argument for distributive justice in which equals ought to be treated equally (and unequals should be treated unequally). He differentiated between distributive justice and rectificatory justice (through which inequalities would be rectified to form just proportions). In more contemporary society that is structured less hierarchically, Rawls has suggested that justice should be based on the liberty principle and the difference principle. Using the concept of the "veil of ignorance," Rawls suggested that we should develop principles of justice in society without knowing, or being concerned about, how we individually would benefit from the system. He argued that we would not be acting from a position of vested interest but from a non-consequentialist golden rule perspective. He further argued that we would maximize social justice by providing equal access for all persons to basic liberties (e.g. freedom of speech) and privileges (such as the right to own property). The difference principle allows that a society can supplement the equality of liberty by democratically agreeing to license individuals to be different and to have special powers, when it is in the best interest of all society to do so. Thus, physicians may write prescriptions, judges may dispense justice and teachers may assign grades because the general population accepts the need to override its own liberty to do these things for its own welfare.

The issue of justice faces us at every turn. At some theoretical level you probably support the idea that a just society is one in which all people have equal access to scarce resources, equal opportunity to participate in any endeavor and in which they will receive equal treatment under the law. Now let's put to the test the question of how just society should be by conducting case study exercises.

Justice and Equality in Education, Sport and Health Care
Exercise 6-5: Gender Equality or Reverse Discrimination?

"A prominent university in the state of Virginia is eliminating men's gymnastics and wrestling and is adding softball as a varsity sport for women. The rationale given by the Athletic Director for cutting the men's sports is that all avenues for increasing revenue have been exhausted, but that funding is just not adequate to continue to offer those sports and to meet the mandate of Title IX. The basic principle of Title IX is that of proportionality. This means that in the interests of social justice and gender equity, funding should be apportioned between men's and women's programs at levels proportionate to the ratio of men to women at the university. The coaches and athletes of the teams that are to be eliminated are incensed that they must bear the burden of this decision. They are threatening to bring a lawsuit against the university based on the principle of reverse discrimination."

1. Use this scenario as a basis for your consideration of distributive v corrective justice (Aristotle) and the liberty v difference principle (Rawls). Reach your own conclusion about the rightness of redistributing scarce resources in university athletics by answering the following questions:

   A. Do you support the basic principle of <u>distributive</u> justice underlying Title IX that women should have equal access, opportunity and treatment?

   B. Given that men have had the lion's share of athletic resources in the past, do you approve of the <u>corrective</u> justice of reallocating a share of these resources to women's athletics in accordance with the proportionality principle of Title IX?

   C. Given that you were at <u>liberty</u> to determine how resources were allocated (but that because of the veil of ignorance you were able to wipe the slate of history clean and not know how you would benefit personally), would you give equal allocations of resources to men's and women's sports?

D. To whom would you give the power to make a <u>difference</u>? Would you give special powers to determine who should receive funding to the legislature, college presidents, athletic directors or some other entity?

Take the time to formulate your position on social justice that is coherent from question to question. Next, we will test your position for consistency to see if it applies to the following scenario taken from the realm of health care. In this case you are asked not only to consider the issue of social justice, but also to use the ethical decision-making process to determine the course of action you should take.

Exercise 6-6: The Priest, the Prostitute and the Parasite

"As the ranking physician in the Emergency Room of St. Joseph's Hospital, you had been counting your blessings that this Sunday night shift had been unusually quiet, when your peace was shattered by the carnage caused by a local automobile accident. Apparently, a young priest had been driving through the downtown area on the way home from his parish when an elderly drunk indigent staggered from the curb into the path of the car. After striking the drunk, the priest's car careened across the road to strike a bystander, a prostitute, before coming to rest, abruptly, against a telephone pole. The first patient brought into the emergency room was the drunk (an individual vilified locally as a parasite on society), closely followed by the prostitute and the priest. Upon closer inspection it quickly becomes apparent to you that they are all close to death and they all need treatment to survive. This treatment is a liver transplant. Unfortunately, you only have one replacement liver available, so you have to make a choice."

In this instance you have to act on your principles of social justice. You are again faced with a case of the allocation of scarce resources, but in this case yours is an urgent life and death decision. We will activate the ethical decision-making process to help you to choose your course of action. I will propose some positions, but in each category, the choice is yours to select the most authentic solution. In the heat of the moment you are assailed by the cries of pain, the sights of suffering and the entreaties of patients and their families. In the emergency room setting, it is difficult to recognize that there are ethical choices to be made (<u>reacting</u>), to disassociate yourself from the clamor (<u>self-distancing</u>) and to pinpoint the particular ethical issues that confront you (<u>identifying</u>). Yet, as you reflect on this predicament you realize that in this case you are responsible for determining social justice, you must decide which potential recipient is most deserving of the potentially life-saving scarce resource. To whom do you give the liver? Your <u>analysis</u> of this predicament presents you with a range of alternatives including distributing the scarce resource on a first come/first serve basis or selecting the recipient who most deserves the life-sustaining treatment.

Step 1. List the alternative courses of action here.

Step 2. Identify the ethical base of your approach to this decision. Will you focus on the goodness of the consequence (<u>teleological</u>) or the <u>rightness</u> of the action (<u>deontological</u>)? _____

If you take a teleological position, will you take the lifestyle of the potential recipient into account? For example are you going to choose the young priest who is deeply involved in caring for his flock over the prostitute and parasite who contribute little to the welfare of society? If you adopt a deontological stance, how will you differentiate between competing right actions, such as responding to the first emergency first, treating a young woman who has her life before her or healing the spiritual healer? Use the ethical decision-making chart (Exercise 3) to help you to analyze the teleological and deontological nature of the alternatives you generate.

Step 3. The culmination of the process is to synthesize your ideal solution and, in a real-life situation, to act upon that decision. Although you are not aware of many personality and predicament factors in this scenario, use the "Synthesizing the Ideal Moral Choice" chart in Exercise 4 to list moderating influences that could affect your decision. For example, consider the influence of your own religious disposition (ethical orientation), your conviction that all human beings are created equal and therefore deserve equal caring attention (moral development) or the misgivings that you have entertained in your later years about drunkenness and prostitution (age-demographic profile). Similarly, list factors in the predicament that might modify your decision. For example, would it make a difference

- that you were friends with the parents of the prostitute (significant others),

- that the drunk had bequeathed a secured trust to the hospital before he succumbed to the bottle (impact) or

- that a previous attending physician who had now risen to the position of hospital administrator had advised you that the way things were done around here was to always take care of the patients with insurance first (ideological climate)?

Finally, let us once again address the issue of social justice. Is the stance that you adopted in this scenario compatible with your conclusion on Title IX? The ultimate goal of the ethical decision-making process is to help you to define a series of compatible positions that constitute your own coherent philosophy of action. If you find that your positions on different ethical issues are contradictory, return to the analysis and synthesis stages of the ethical decision-making process to differentiate between the positions and to resolve questions about these differences. In this case, ask yourself what is different about the allocation of scarce resources in sport from medicine. This process of reevaluation completes the cycle of ethical decision-making by taking you back to reflect on first principles such as justice and equality, or freedom and responsibility and your position in regard to them.

Individual Autonomy and Paternalism

The concept of justice is connected to issues of freedom in that legislation is often geared toward curbing or facilitating individual liberties. In health and medicine, sport and education, so many ethical dilemmas hinge on our perception of the roles and responsibilities of individuals to themselves and to their society that we will address the question of individual autonomy and paternalism here.

A premise of a free and democratic society is that we have individual liberty. In America, such liberties singled out by the Constitution are the freedom of speech, religious expression and the right to bear arms. However, the concept of personal freedom is framed within the boundaries of public accountability. For example, we may be free to carry arms (in certain circumstances) but we are not free to use those arms to hurt others (except in certain circumstances). One of the constraints placed upon our liberty is the legal limitation of laws designed to specify the nature of and limits of our freedom. But, in many circumstances that we face daily, there are no legal mandates, only our personal sense of the right course of action. You will face the relationship of individual autonomy and paternalism frequently from both sides of the issue, (in such contexts as a parent or a child, a student or a teacher, a coach or an athlete, a patient or a health care provider). Consequently, it is important that we attempt to develop a philosophy of action for our use in both circumstances. It should be consistent in its premises and coherent in its application. We will develop and test such a philosophy by addressing various contemporary issues. First, we will develop a theory of freedom by considering:

Exercise 6-7: Procreative Profit

"Female students at elite colleges around the nation are facing a new invitation. In the want ad columns of the student newspapers they are encountering messages requesting that they sell their eggs to deserving couples. Of course, they must meet certain physiological criteria (e.g. tall, blonde, blue-eyed), they must be intelligent and have no history of psychological disorders. The rewards for undergoing the necessary surgical procedures can be considerable. If qualifying coeds are willing to sign up with the top agents, they can command up to $50,000 dollars for their services."

Step 1.   Assume that you read such an advertisement and that you fall into the category of eligibility. Reacting entails that responding to this invitation has ethical implications. Self-distancing entails overcoming strong emotional and engrained responses. Identifying philosophical premises includes you in the process of defining the nature and parameters of your personal freedom.

Step 2.   Analyze the ethical bases for your decision. From a teleological perspective, positive consequences might include profit and helping couples who can't have their own children (maybe). Alternatively, you may want to avoid the consequences of diluting our gene pool and the problems of eugenic selection. Deontological analysis involves laws of the land, rules from religion and social contract issues of treating others as you would wish to be treated into the determination of the rightness of this course of action. Use the chart from Exercise 3 to express your own teleological and deontological positions.

Step 3.   Use the ideal solution, that you developed through the process of analysis and synthesis, to develop a definition of freedom. This definition should incorporate a description of what you feel free to do and what limits you place on your own freedom. It should generalize your notion of liberty to circumstances beyond the Procreative Profit scenario. It should also be an authentic expression of your notion of liberty that extends beyond the circumscribed boundaries of that scenario that may not have applied to you. If you choose, you can complete your definition of freedom by filling in the blanks in the following statement: "I feel free to _____(action)_____ except when it _____(limits)_____. Next, we will test this definition by introducing the influence of authority into the mix by considering:

Exercise 6-8: Freedom From Testing

"A major problem in elite sports today is the influence of performance-enhancing drugs. Consequently, governing bodies, such as the International Olympic Congress and the National Collegiate Athletic Association have instituted drug-testing procedures to control the situation. Some athletes have condemned this practice as being an unreasonable invasion of their privacy. They are particularly concerned about testing for drugs that might be classified as restorative (necessary to restore an athlete to a "normal" competitive level, such as asthma medication) or recreational (drugs that athletes may choose to take for leisure that have no proven performance-enhancing effect, such as marijuana or cocaine)."

Assume that you are a) an elite athlete who has been asked to submit to drug testing and b) an athletic director who is responsible for drug testing at a college. Your responses to the scenario may vary widely in these two roles, so record your responses separately. At the conclusion of this exercise compare your responses to determine where they converge and where they diverge.

Step 1.   Reacting involves recognizing that by submitting to(athlete) or implementing (A.D.) a drug test you are also submitting to or implementing a paternalistic act. Paternalism is the implementation of authority in the best interests of the athlete and athletics. Implicit in this act is the ethical premise that this course of action is the right course of action based upon an appropriate relationship between athlete and administrator. Self-distancing entails overcoming the natural revulsion caused by the process of passing urine in public or of testing body fluids through injection. Identification involves the recognition of the philosophic issues such as

- privacy (of the athlete's person),

- concerns about performance-enhancing drugs (such as that it is not natural, it coerces other athletes to do the same, it can be harmful to the athlete, it creates an unfair advantage)

- freedom of choice that is violated by testing for substances that do not enhance performance

Identify the ethical issues that you see in this scenario and prioritize them before proceeding to the second step.

Step 2.   Analyzing drug testing involves asking what consequences you are seeking and how best to reach them (teleological) and determining the rightness of the course of action as measured by legislation, secular codes, religious creeds and universal intuitive laws (deontological). As an athlete, you may be most interested in the consequence of your performance and in the freedom to maximize it, or you may be most concerned that you be seen to follow the rules and regulations. As an administrator you may seek the consequence of preserving the level playing field. From deontological perspectives, you may be concerned that the laws of the land concerning the illegal use of drugs, or the code of the governing bodies regarding performance-enhancing drugs be observed. The gray area that requires further interpretation is the issue of performance-enhancers that are not banned (such as creatine and androstenine by some organizations) or drugs that are restorative or recreational in nature. Describe your ethical premise from both perspectives and the courses of action you might follow based on that premise here_____

_____

_____.

Step 3.   Synthesizing the most ideal solution entails determining when and under what conditions individual freedom can justifiably be curbed by paternalistic action. Your ethical orientation may lead you to adopt a particular religious creed that prohibits the use of drugs or to obediently acknowledge that "the law is the law and that's the end of the matter." Alternatively you may live by more libertarian standards that permit more freedom of choice. If you are at the pre-conventional level of cognitive moral developments, you may tend to act to further your own success. If you are at a higher stage, you may be more concerned with the integrity of the sports event. Such features as your age and gender of your demographic profile will be influential. Issues related to your predicament may radically affect your actions. For example,

- if you happen to be on the verge of a world record (impact)

- or you know that your family is depending upon you to earn a living through your performance (significant others),

- or you know that every other athlete is using (ideological climate), you may approach this ethical dilemma quite differently.

Use the chart from exercise 5 to assess the personality and predicament factors that would influence your ideal solution.

Exercise 6-9: Intrusive Paternalism

"John, a forty year old college professor, was enjoying a warm light-wind summer day on Lake Winnepausakee. An expert windsurfer, he was staying close to the beach so that he could display his skills to his young family. Although no one on the beach was particularly interested in his windsurfing prowess, all eyes did turn his way when a coast guard power-boat drew up next to his board with its blue light flashing. Having been told to drop his sail, John was informed that he was breaking the law by not wearing a personal flotation device and that he would have to pay a $20 fine. John's entreaties that he was an expert, that the conditions were mild and that he would take responsibility for his own actions fell on deaf ears. A splendid day of windsurfing ended in ignominy as John was towed to the beach looking quite abject and forlorn to respond to the questions and derision of the onlookers."

Before you embark upon the ethical decision-making process, consider how this scenario differs from the Procreative Profit and Freedom from Testing case studies. In John Stuart Mill's famous discussion of anti-paternalism in <u>On Liberty</u>, the conditions for freedom of choice and action are clearly articulated. Mill argued that providing an individual is mature, rational and fully informed of the risks there should be no limitation placed upon a freely chosen course of action. In all three case studies, moral choices were made by adults who were rational and who were fully informed of the risks of their action. However, Mill also placed one caveat upon his libertarian position: the harm principle. He concluded that the only reason for authority to intrude upon the freedom of an individual is to prevent harm to others. In other words it would be insufficient cause to stop John from windsurfing to prevent harm to himself, but it could have been justified to prevent harm to others. If you accept Mill's position, the issue that you must resolve is what constitutes "harm." Is the possibility of a collision or the expense of a potential search and rescue or the unlikely occurrence of a drowning incident sufficient justification for the Coast Guards action?

Step 1. At this point, you should have enough information to develop and articulate a philosophical position on the relationship of individual freedom and institutional paternalism. State your position here _____

_____.

Step 2.   Re-evaluate your position by checking that it does apply in each of the three case studies in this section.

Step 3.   Consider your position in this philosophic principle as it relates to the stance you have previously articulated on justice and equality. Are the two positions coherent or do you notice some internal inconsistencies that make them contradictory?

The process of developing critical thinking skills and a coherent philosophy entails resolving such issues as those presented in the case study by referring back to a basic core of beliefs on such key philosophic principles as justice and equality, freedom and paternalism. The process is a lifelong endeavor of evaluating and re-evaluating ethical decisions, defining and refining the theoretical premises and philosophic principles that govern your behavior. The ultimate goal of this journey is to develop a philosophy that will help you to choose the morally right path to living "the good life."

Conclusion: Live the Good Life

The culmination of the philosophic process in general and the ethical decision-making process in particular is the good life. The sort of critical thinking that you have engaged in throughout this book creates the examined life that is worth living. The emphasis on ethics in this chapter will facilitate living the life that is good in terms of the moral choices you will make.

The meaning of the good life is a matter of individual interpretation and moral choice. As we have seen earlier in this chapter, the definition of life is fraught with problems. Ethical issues such as euthanasia and physician assisted suicide revolve around the question. Clearly if the moment of death is when the brain ceases to operate, that places a different set of constraints upon the physician than if the termination of life is when all physiological functions cease to be viable (even with technological intervention). The issue of the sanctity of life versus the quality of life that is the premise of these debates is applicable to all of us. The sanctity of life argument is that life, even at its most minimal level must be preserved, whereas quality of life advocates argue that the wishes of the patient facing the debilitating processes of pain and decrepitude should be honored. Similarly, life for the healthy may be little more than a process of survival, or it may have the quality of the good life. In other words, we can focus on adding years to our life or on adding life to our years.

Choosing the good life entails making moral choices about the meaning of happiness. Happiness is the basic ingredient of the good life. Human happiness can be hedonistic. It can revolve around the satiation of your own appetites. Or happiness can be utilitarian in nature. A search for the good life can revolve around the greatest happiness principle, which involves acting in such a way that you will create the greatest happiness for the greatest number. As we have seen in the discussion of personality factors in ethical decision-making, the hedonistic approach tends to be associated with precognitive moral development, whereas the more altruistic and benevolent interpretations of happiness represent a higher level of moral maturity.

To return to the recurring theme of human movement that is the focus of this book, the approach to the good life that you will take in the game of life is analogous to the happiness you desire from sport itself. In many ways, sport is a microcosm. As you play, you display your ethics in action. A hedonistic approach to sport is premised upon self-promotion. The purpose of participation is to win, both in the score and in terms of social standing and material benefits. Hedonistic decision-making tends to be teleological. The ends justify the means. Sport is an exercise in manipulation, using others as the means to reach the desired ends. Alternatively, happiness in sport defined in utilitarian terms embraces the welfare of other participants and the game itself as well as the pursuit of personal pleasure. The treatment of others in the play setting is more supportive than it is exploitative. An element of mutual respect and a willingness to abide by the unwritten code of sportsmanship characterize the quality of sport participation that will lead to the greatest happiness principle. Similarly the game of life can be played at the hedonistic level. You can seek personal gratification, often at the expense of others, and through processes of manipulation and exploitation, seek to get ahead, to be #1 in your professional and personal life. Or, you can focus more on the utilitarian process than on the end product of living. In this case you will seek to benefit only when the gain is mutual and you will respect those you interact with as you strive to promote the greatest happiness principle. Ultimately, your definition of the good life is a product of your moral choices.

Review

In this chapter we have encountered the "hottest" area of philosophy today. Ethics is universally recognized as being essential to guide, and in some cases to counter, emerging trends in society. Of particular interest to us is the need for ethics in the realms of health and human movement, as well as in our own personal growth and development. This need for ethics is more specifically a need to recognize and cope with the ethical dilemmas that we face daily. The ethical decision-making process outlined in this chapter is an approach that you can take to enhancing your skills in making moral choices. The final section of this chapter is focussed on applications of this decision-making process to the two basic issues of justice/equality and individual autonomy/paternalism in the realms of health and human movement. The culmination of the chapter, and indeed of the whole book, is the contribution that these skills have in helping you to seek happiness through living "the good life." Living the good life entails more than living your life as play and seeking beauty in all that you do. It also pivots on the ethical decisions that you make to define the happiness that you seek. The final section of this book has provided a perspective and a procedure that will help you to choose the right path through life now and in your future. In this book you have used a framework for finding meaning that can serve you well for years after you no longer encounter texts in classrooms.